LOST MYSTERIES

HISTORY'S GREATEST SECRETS, LEGENDS & HIDDEN TREASURES

PAIGE TOWLER

kids
HEARST
HOME

CONTENTS

UNCOVER THE SECRETS OF THE PAST

To read more about the mystery surrounding Nefertiti (depicted here), an ancient Egyptian queen, see page 136.

In an age where scientific advances happen in the blink of an eye and explorers scour every inch of the globe (and even into space!), it may seem like we have uncovered everything there is to know. But the truth is, the world is teeming with mysteries: Many incredible people, extraordinary places, even top secret treasures have been lost to history! From missing hordes of jewels to vanished tombs, from what life was like millions of years ago to how humans came to be, and from sunken cities to the real stories behind legends and myths, there is so much left to discover.

Lucky for us, explorations and discoveries by scientists and researchers are bringing us closer than ever to solving some of the greatest lost mysteries. Read on to learn how paleontologists decoded **dinosaur secrets** (p. 10) and unearthed early human ancestors (p. 16). Find out how archaeologists have revealed **tombs** buried deep in sands (p. 40), and how engineers have shed light on **shipwrecks** hidden at the bottom of the sea (p. 88). And get the latest info on how historians and other experts are working to solve other mysteries, like what happened to Amelia Earhart (p. 124); whether the lost city of El Dorado really existed (p. 150); and where the **missing treasure** of the Amber Room could be (p. 130).

Of course, some of these searches have only exposed more mysteries: What happened to the **powerful civilizations** that once ruled the jungles of Guatemala (p. 104)? Did prehistoric animals dig enormous networks of caves (p. 22)? And was King Arthur a real person (p. 148)? Read on to learn about some of the most **incredible mysteries** still puzzling experts around the world—and decide for yourself!

As you flip through the pages in this book, you'll encounter cool history, fun facts, and Take It Further questions and activities meant to help you dive deeper into the unknown. So, what are you waiting for? You're on the case!

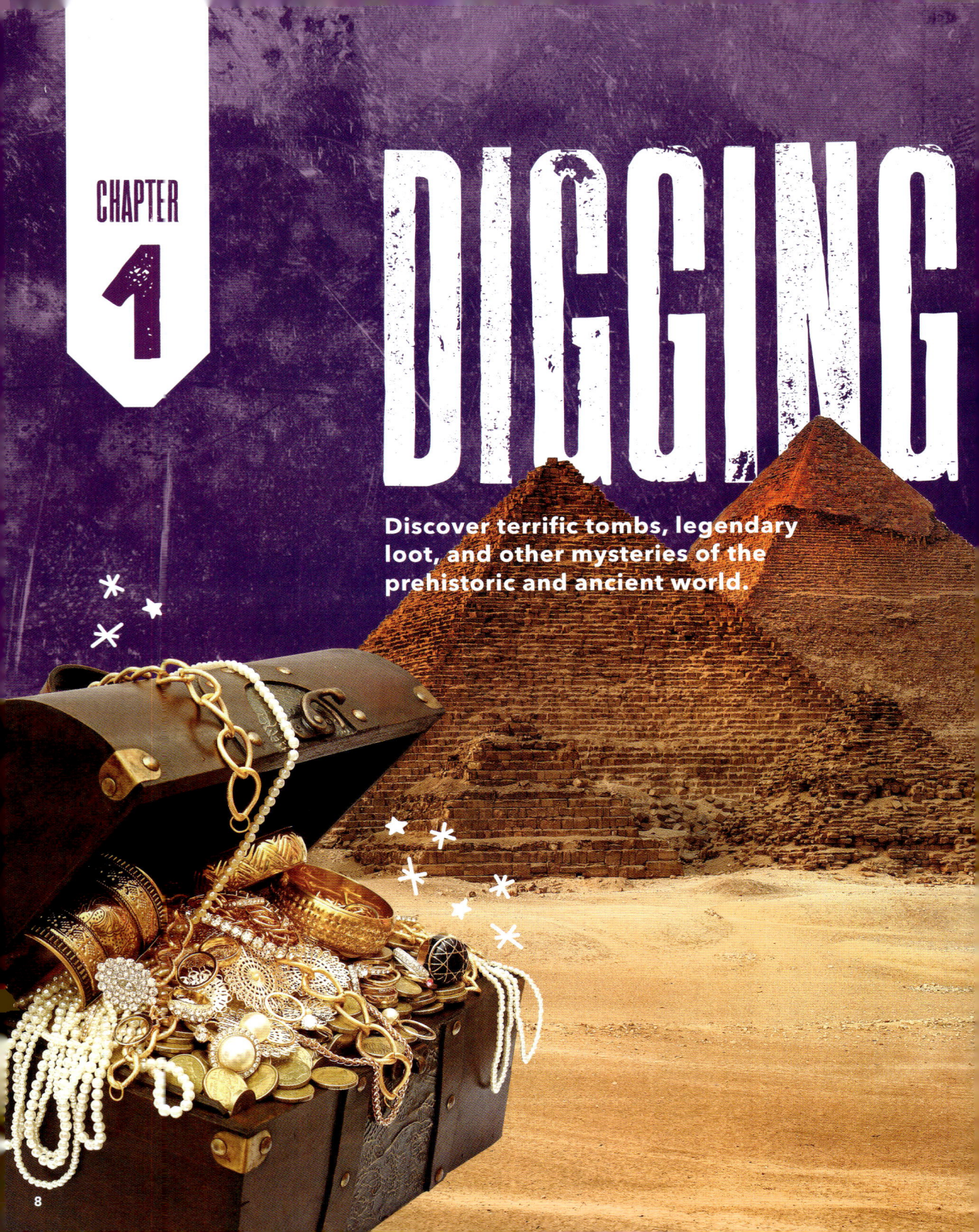

CHAPTER 1

DIGGING

Discover terrific tombs, legendary loot, and other mysteries of the prehistoric and ancient world.

UP THE PAST

DINOSAUR DISCOVERIES

THE LOST REPTILES

Dinosaur discoverers in the past imagined a time when savage sea serpents terrorized the oceans and *Iguanodon* with rhinoceros-like horns stalked the lands. They described a dinosaur that stored its brain in its rear end, and another whose head was at the end of its tail. Today, these incredible-sounding dinosaurs and prehistoric reptiles are lost to history—because they never actually existed. But for a long time, people thought they did!

For nearly 200 million years, enormous reptiles, including those known as dinosaurs, did roam Earth. Most dinosaurs—except for avian dinosaurs and their bird descendants—went extinct some 66 million years ago, leaving only their preserved remains and traces, or fossils. Today, scientists use special methods and advanced technologies to study these fossils. But for most of history, people didn't have access to those tools. In fact, it wasn't until the 1800s that experts began to treat fossil discoveries scientifically.

Exactly what dinosaurs and other prehistoric creatures looked like remains a mystery. But illustrations like these of a *Tyrannosaurus rex* (left), *Iguanodon* (right), and pterosaurs (ancient flying reptiles, upper right) were created based on the evidence and clues that paleontologists and other scientists had discovered at that time.

An image of an *Iguanodon* based on a drawing created in 1910 (left); An illustration of British geologist William Buckland (right).

In this illustration, paleontologist Gideon Mantell displays fossilized *Iguanodon* teeth (below).

In 1818, British geologist William Buckland was studying a large collection of fossils with French zoologist Georges Cuvier when they realized that dinosaur bones were similar to those of a modern lizard. Buckland called the discovery *Megalosaurus*, "giant lizard." Then, in 1822, British scientist Mary Ann Mantell came upon what looked like an enormous reptile tooth. She and her geologist husband, Gideon Mantell, recognized that the tooth was similar to an iguana's tooth. They named this mysterious animal *Iguanodon*, or "iguana tooth."

By the 1840s, paleontology, or the study of fossils, was becoming more popular. A British scientist named Richard Owen believed that the species people kept discovering must be related to each other. He came up with a name for them: *Dinosauria*, meaning "monstrous lizard." Soon, paleontologists around the world were clamoring to find fossils and learn more about dinosaurs. But lots of mistakes would be made along the journey to discovery.

MASSIVE MISTAKES

Things came to a head in the 1860s. Two esteemed American paleontologists, Edward Cope and Othniel Marsh, were on the hunt for as many dinosaur fossils as they could find. Though the pair had started as friends, they quickly grew into bitter rivals trying to outdo—and even sabotage—each other. In their haste to find and identify fossils as quickly as possible, they began to make some strange errors. In 1868, Cope discovered the *Elasmosaurus*, and triumphantly displayed a reconstruction. But as Marsh (perhaps also triumphantly) pointed out, Cope had constructed the dinosaur's spine backward, so its head was now on its tail! But Marsh wasn't without fault. In 1877, he incorrectly proposed the idea that the *Stegosaurus* had two brains: one in its head and one in its rear end.

The more the scientists compared fossils to modern reptiles, the better idea they had of what dinosaurs might have looked like. However, that doesn't mean that they stopped making mistakes. For example, many 20th-century experts believed that dinosaurs were smooth or scaly. But thanks to ongoing discoveries, scientists now know that many dinosaurs had feathers! As science changes, the future may hold more dinosaur discoveries—and perhaps even some more "lost" dinosaur species.

Today, paleontologists believe that many dinosaurs—like this fighting pair of dromaeosaurids—had feathers.

FUN FACT

The iconic *Brontosaurus*, perhaps one of the most famous dinosaurs, was an enormous plant-eater with a long neck. The species was first discovered by Othniel Marsh in 1879.

FANTASTIC DINOSAUR FEATURES

Check out some of the most *dinomite* dinosaurs with incredible, unusual, and surprising characteristics.

BIGGEST BITE

Tyrannosaurus rex
is often called the king of the dinosaurs, and with good reason. This predator packed a beastly bite! *T. rex* had teeth that could reach up to 12 inches (30.5 cm) long—about as long as an adult's forearm. The bite of a *T. rex* was the strongest of any land animal. In fact, being bitten by a *Tyrannosaurus* rex would have been about the same as being crushed by its who e body. Long live the king!

FANCIEST FRILL

Some 76 million years ago, **Kosmoceratops** sported a frill at the top of its head that included 15 horns and spikes, with some horns even folding downward in a fan shape. Scientists think *Kosmoceratops* used this headgear to attract mates. How dashing!

TALL TAILS

Stegouros had a tail that was a handy weapon. Covered in bladelike bony growths, it looked like a deadly blade called the *macuahuitl* that the ancient Aztec of Central America later invented. Scientists think that *Stegouros* would swing its tail to defend against attacking predators.

TERRIFYING TEETH

Majungasaurus was a predatory dinosaur that lived between 66 and 70 million years ago. It had a mouthful of teeth that were constantly regrowing, similar to a shark's. Scientists think that when food was scarce, this deadly dinosaur would turn its teeth on its own kind, attacking and eating other *Majungasaurus*. Talk about a terrible lunch guest!

COOL CLAWS

Therizinosaurus had long, curving claws that could grow more than 3.3 feet (1 m)—about the length of a baseball bat. However, scientists think that this dinosaur was an herbivore, meaning it probably didn't use its claws for slashing. The claws also may have been too delicate to do much damage in self-defense. Instead, the claws likely helped attract mates.

LOST HUMANS OF HISTORY

Since ancient times, we've created myths and stories to answer the question: Where do we come from? By the 19th century, however, scientists began to turn their minds toward the natural world to explain our origins. In 1871, the English scientist Charles Darwin published a controversial book called *On the Origin of Species* claiming that animals—including humans—evolved, or changed, over time. In fact, Darwin even suggested that humans and other apes, such as chimpanzees, had descended from a common ancestor long ago.

Soon, paleontologists began to unearth fossils that supported Darwin's idea. In 1891, Dutch scientists discovered the fossil of an early human species known as *Homo erectus*. In 1974, scientists found the three-million-year-old fossil of one of the oldest known human relatives, *Australopithecus afarensis*, or Lucy, in Ethiopia.

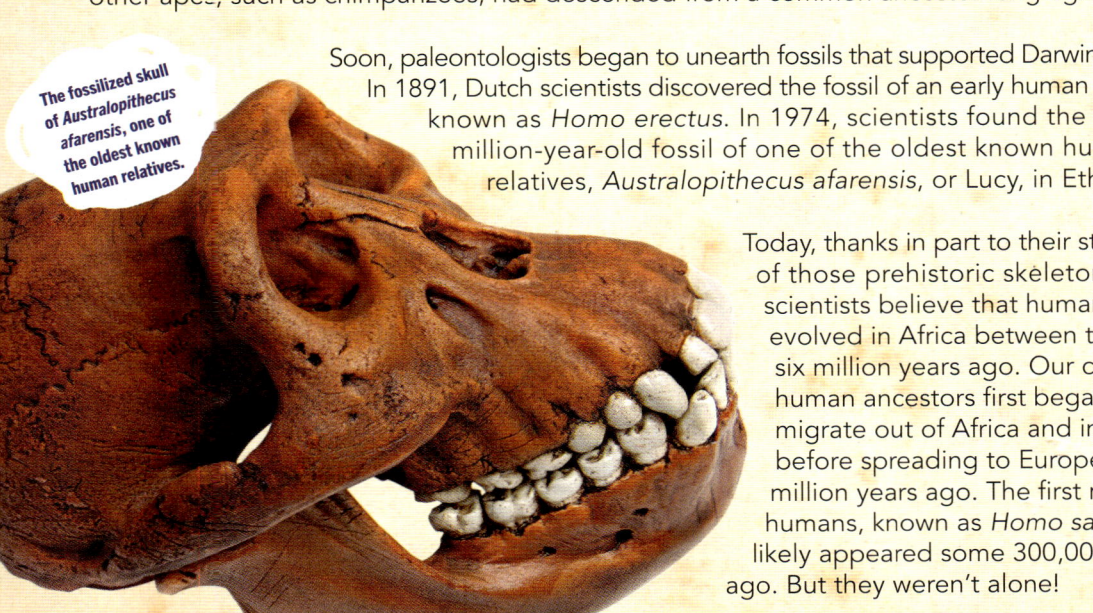

The fossilized skull of *Australopithecus afarensis*, one of the oldest known human relatives.

Today, thanks in part to their studies of those prehistoric skeletons, scientists believe that humans first evolved in Africa between two and six million years ago. Our closest human ancestors first began to migrate out of Africa and into Asia before spreading to Europe two million years ago. The first modern humans, known as *Homo sapiens*, likely appeared some 300,000 years ago. But they weren't alone!

This re-creation shows what researchers think Lucy may have looked like.

Another type of species known as *Homo neanderthalensis*, or the Neanderthals, also appeared around 400,000 years ago. But then they disappeared some 40,000 years ago. What happened? Scientists have several theories.

It's possible that *Homo sapiens* drove Neanderthals into extinction—perhaps through direct fighting, or by competition for food and living places. Others think that disease may have wiped out the Neanderthals. Or that over the years, Neanderthals had a harder time surviving the world's changing climate. For now, the truth remains a mystery.

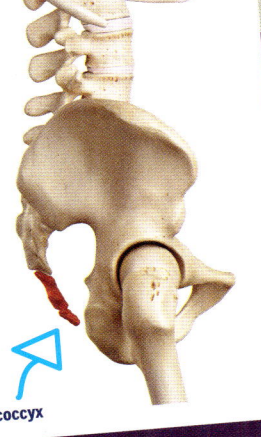

coccyx

Telling Tails

Scientist think that, like monkeys, our ancestors had tails! Animals that spend most of their time on four legs often have tails to help stay balanced. But our early primate ancestors slowly evolved to walk upright on two legs, meaning they likely no longer needed a tail to balance. Over time, their tails got shorter and shorter. Today, the only remnant of these ancient tails is a bone on the end of our spine called the coccyx (pronounced "KAHK-siks").

A MAMMOTH MARVEL

The world was very different for humans living 15,000 years ago. On average, it was about 11 degrees colder than it is today. Because of this, ice sheets covered nearly a third of Earth's land. Not only was the land different, but Earth's animals were also built very different from the animals of today.

Enter the mighty woolly mammoth. First appearing about 300,000 years ago, these elephant-like creatures with long, shaggy fur were well suited to cold weather. Their ears were relatively small compared to their body size, which helped stop heat from leaving their bodies. Woolly mammoths also had enormous, 15-foot (4.6-m)-long tusks that they used to dig for grasses buried beneath the snow. However, some 10,000 years ago, woolly mammoths went extinct, likely due to a warming climate that caused much of the vegetation to die or change. The giants were lost to history. Or were they?

A 3D rendering of a woolly mammoth skeleton.

In 2007, a reindeer herder of the Nenets people of Siberia, Russia, made an incredible discovery. There, on the bank of a river, was a nearly perfectly preserved mammoth calf. The calf weighed about the size of a newborn elephant, and the small hairs on her body were still visible. How was this possible? As it turned out, the calf had died more than 40,000 years before when she seemingly fell into a mud pit. Scientists think that the mud was full of unique bacteria that produced a chemical called lactic acid. This chemical mummified the calf's body, keeping away other destructive microorganisms.

The permafrost, or frozen ground, that had hidden the calf's body had melted, revealing the pristine mummy. This baby mammoth mummy—now named Lyuba after the herder's wife—had so many secrets to share. Scientists were able to study her teeth and organs, and even the grass meal that was still in her stomach. They were also able to learn more about how mammoth calves lived and ate, and scientists hope to solve even more mysteries about these lost animals.

TAKE IT FURTHER

What do you think would happen if scientists brought back a previously extinct species? How do you think the species could survive in a world that is very different from the one it lived in?

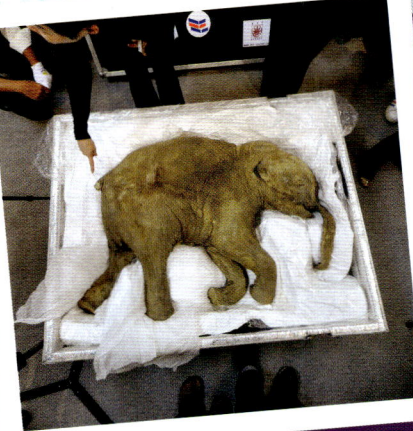

Return of the Mammoth

Today, scientists continue to discover frozen mammoth mummies like Lyuba. These mummified woolly mammoth bodies sometimes still contain preserved flesh and blood, which means that scientists can study their genetic material, or DNA. Some scientists want to find a way to combine woolly mammoth DNA with that of one of the animal's modern-day relatives—the Asian elephant—to create a new, living species. This animal wouldn't exactly be a woolly mammoth, but it would be something very close . . . a mammophant!

FROZEN IN TIME

Thanks to subzero temperatures, Lyuba isn't the only incredible frosted discovery from the past. Check out these amazing finds.

FROZEN FOAL

The mummy of a 42,000-year-old horse was so well preserved that scientists were able to draw its blood. They hope to use it to study the horse's DNA, and there's even talk of trying to clone it to resurrect the now extinct species. Giddyap!

ANCIENT MICROBES

Scientists have discovered ancient microbes and bacteria—some more than 48,000 years old—frozen in glaciers, permafrost, and ice sheets. They've even been able to revive some of these microbes to study how they behave

SIBERIAN ICE MAIDEN

The frozen mummy of a woman who lived in what is now Siberia, Russia, some 2,400 years ago is so well preserved that you can still see the reindeer tattoo on her left shoulder. Now *that's* permanent!

Re-creation of the tattoo on the frozen mummy's shoulder!

DOGOR THE WOLF PUP

One wolf pup that died 18,000 years ago was so well preserved that you can see its fur, nose, whiskers, eyelashes, and teeth.

ÖTZI THE ICEMAN

In 1991, hikers discovered the frozen mummy of a man who had died more than 5,000 years ago in the Alps mountain range between Austria and Italy.

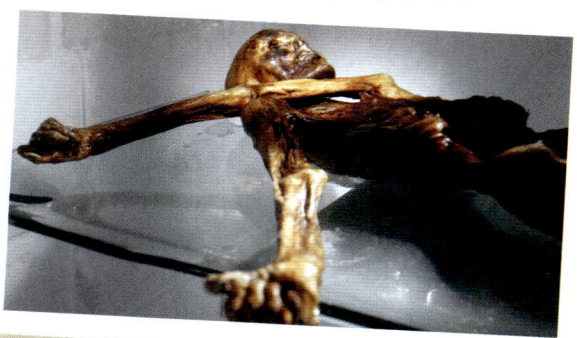

SECRET TUNNEL MAKERS

In 2010, a Brazilian geologist named Amilcar Adamy heard rumors of an incredible cave system at the border of Brazil and Bolivia. Apparently, a local farmer had been driving his tractor when the vehicle suddenly sank deep into the soil. As it turned out, the tractor had broken through the roof of an enormous cavern. When Adamy arrived to investigate, he was shocked by what he found.

It was a system of tunnels, all right, but the tunnels—which were tall and wide enough for multiple adults to walk through upright side by side—didn't look like any natural formation Adamy had seen before. The walls were too smooth and round.

Doedicurus was a prehistoric glyptodont—a giant mammal similar to armadillos.

On its hind legs, the extinct ground sloth would have stretched twice as tall as an adult human!

They were also covered in large scratch marks. And as Adamy would soon find out, similar tunnels had been discovered all over Brazil, and even in other South American countries. Elsewhere in Brazil, geologist Heinrich Frank was studying another system of tunnels with smooth, rounded walls and the same claw marks.

As Frank and Adamy continued to investigate, they became more and more convinced: Animals had carved these tunnels. But not just any animals—enormous, prehistoric creatures that lived more than 10,000 years ago. To figure out which animals carved these paleoburrows, as they are called, Frank narrowed down the search to prehistoric animals with large claws—after all, the animals certainly wouldn't have been using chisels or hammers. This left two suspects: giant ground sloths and giant armadillos! Scientists believe that giant armadillos, which grew to be the size of cars, likely carved out the smaller of the tunnels. That means that giant ground sloths—prehistoric sloths that could reach the size of today's African elephants—formed the largest of the tunnels. Frank believes that many generations of animals carved the tunnels over hundreds or even thousands of years. But why? That remains a mystery—for now.

Sloth Secrets

Giant ground sloths may be a thing of the past, but their presence can still be seen in nature—and not just in the enormous paleoburrows. Scientists think that without giant ground sloths, avocados would be extinct. Due to their large seeds, avocados were too bulky for many animals to swallow. But not for enormous ground sloths: They could swallow the fruit whole! The sloths would later disperse the seeds in their poop, causing new trees to grow. By the time sloths and other enormous prehistoric animals went extinct, humans had come to love avocados and grow them on their own. So, the next time you enjoy some guacamole, thank a ground sloth!

SURPRISES OF THE SWAMPS

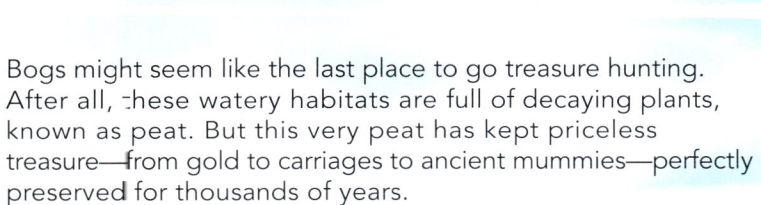

Bogs might seem like the last place to go treasure hunting. After all, these watery habitats are full of decaying plants, known as peat. But this very peat has kept priceless treasure—from gold to carriages to ancient mummies—perfectly preserved for thousands of years.

As peat decays, it releases a type of acid often called bog acid. Rather than breaking things down, this acid helps preserve organic matter—almost like a cucumber pickled in vinegar. On top of that, bogs are found mostly in cold northern climates, meaning the cold water slows down or even halts decay. Because of this, ancient peoples who lived there

This bronze statue depicts the 2,400-year-old body of a man found in a peat bog in Denmark (upper image); A miniature bronze chariot discovered in a former peat bog in Denmark (lower image).

sometimes used bogs as early refrigerators. Archaeologists have found butter and animal fats preserved in Irish bogs for thousands of years—and still good enough to eat today…if anyone is daring enough!

However, bogs were important for other reasons too. Ancient Celtic peoples living in western and central Europe sometimes used bogs as places to give thanks to their gods and goddesses. Their offerings might have included gold and other important objects. A construction worker in Ireland discovered a medieval book that had been thrown into a bog some 1,000 years ago. Archaeologists in Denmark found parts of two elaborately carved iron wagons that had been sacrificed more than 2,000 years ago. Occasionally, the ancient Celts even sacrificed humans in the bogs. A man who was sacrificed about 2,300 years ago in what is now Denmark was so well preserved that archaeologists could study his last meal. What other secrets could bogs be hiding?

Peat in the bogs releases a type of acid that helps preserve organic matter.

KING TUT'S TOMB

INTO THE CRYPT

On November 4, 1922, British archaeologist Howard Carter and his team were digging in the shifting sands of Egypt's Valley of the Kings. Near Luxor, the site was part of the ancient Egyptian city of Thebes, where many important pharaohs had been buried. Most of the site had either been excavated years before or looted by tomb robbers. However, Carter was sure that at least one tomb had yet to be found: that of the young pharaoh King Tutankhamen (or King Tut). Carter had been searching for the tomb for seven years with no results. The man financing the dig, Lord Carnarvon, was ready to cancel the whole operation.

It took several weeks of careful excavation, but by November 26, the team had found steps, and now they were standing at the tomb's doors. The archaeologists carefully made a hole in the doors, allowing Carter to raise a candle and peek inside. The room glinted with golden objects that had been untouched for more than 3,300 years.

The team discovered incredible riches: chariots, thrones, and animal-shaped beds, many covered in gold. Next, they made their way into the burial chamber, where they discovered King Tutankhamen himself, mummified and carefully buried within a series of three golden coffins and a stone sarcophagus. But that wasn't all: The tomb contained two more rooms, both full of thousands of treasures like jewelry, statues, weapons, and more.

Two men stand at the entrance of King Tut's tomb (top). This 1922 photo shows the view inside the tomb once the outer door was knocked down (bottom).

Archaeologists remove a golden shrine from Tutankhamen's tomb (left); Archaeologists carefully transport the various parts of an ancient chariot from the tomb (below).

CURSED!

The discovery of King Tut's tomb was magnificent, but wasn't without trouble. Carter and the Egyptian government argued bitterly over who should "own" the ancient artifacts. Carter even stole several artifacts and jewels, despite the Egyptian government's insistence that they should all remain in Egypt.

That wasn't the last of the troubles. Rumors began to swirl. Some claimed the tomb held a powerful curse that would doom anyone who disturbed it.

Six months after Carter's team opened the tomb, Lord Carnarvon, who financed the dig, suddenly and mysteriously died. Not only that—Carter had gifted one of Tut's artifacts to a friend who then suffered great misfortune in the forms of fires and flood. And within the next several years, other members

This golden bracelet, made some 3,400 years ago, features a large scarab carved from lapis lazuli and various gems.

King Tut's mummy (below) was discovered inside an elaborate sarcophagus (above).

of the archaeological team died unexpectedly. Was the curse real? Today, experts believe that there was no curse—just bad luck and natural deaths. In fact, most believe that Lord Carnarvon died of blood poisoning from an infected mosquito bite. The rest was simple coincidence—helped by an overenthusiastic media, which published the sensational stories in countless newspapers.

TAKE IT FURTHER

Many ancient Egyptians believed that they would be able to bring the items that were buried with them to the afterlife. If you were an ancient Egyptian ruler, what items would you want to bring with you and why?

A Mysterious Mummy

Although the mystery of the mummy's curse has been solved, one important question remains: How did the pharaoh die? At just 19 years old, Tutankhamen was relatively young when he died. He also seemed to have an injured skull and a broken leg. Early theories suggested that King Tut had been murdered by a blow to the head. However, researchers soon realized that the skull "injury" could have been caused while archaeologists unwrapped the mummy—long after Tut had died. Other experts suggested that perhaps Tut had died in a chariot crash, which had also caused the broken leg. Most recently, 3D scans and X-rays of the mummy have suggested that the pharaoh was ill when he passed away. This has led some to speculate that King Tut may have died from an infection resulting from his broken leg.

AMAZING ARTIFACTS OF TUT'S TOMB

From golden coffins to ancient board games, King Tut's tomb was stacked with treasure—both historical and literal. Peek at some of the most amazing finds here.

METEORITE DAGGER

This dagger was made from iron found in a meteorite.

GOLDEN MASK

Weighing more than 20 pounds (9 kg), this death mask is made of gold and semiprecious stones.

COFFINS

King Tut's outer two coffins are made of gold-covered wood. The innermost coffin is made from solid gold. All three show Tut holding the crook and flail, symbols of the ancient Egyptian god Osiris.

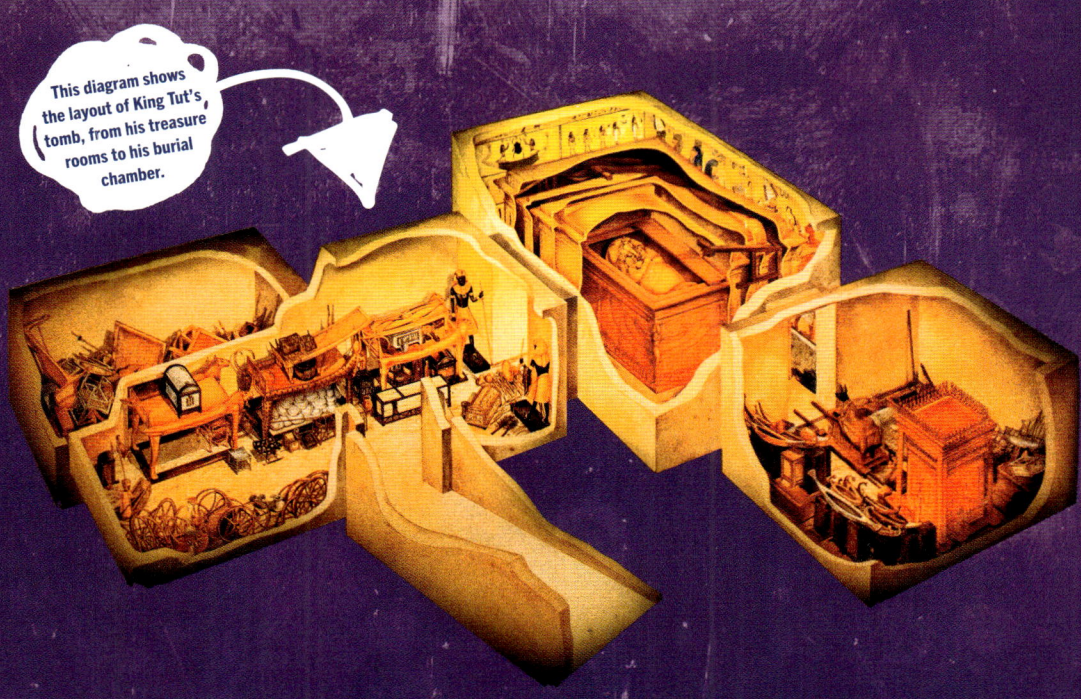

This diagram shows the layout of King Tut's tomb, from his treasure rooms to his burial chamber.

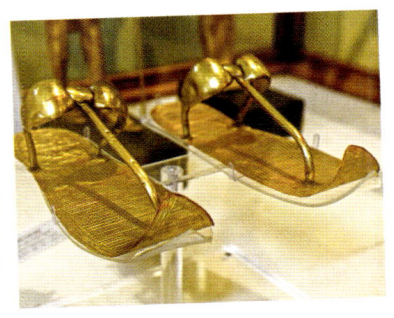

GOLDEN SANDALS
Talk about cool kicks: These sandals are made from thin sheets of pure gold.

CHARIOT
Carter's team found six chariots in the tomb. These chariots may once have had cloth canopies that kept the rider shaded. Now that's riding in luxury!

BOARD GAME
The young king was buried with at least four board games, including one known as senet.

THE NAZCA LINES

In 1926, Peruvian archaeologist Toribio Mejía Xesspe was hiking in southern Peru when he stepped into a ditch. The ditch was strange, though. It was very long. More unusually, it seemed to be man-made. Xesspe continued to investigate. Soon, he realized something incredible: This "ditch" and others nearby were part of ancient geoglyphs, or human-made carvings in the earth. And these particular geoglyphs were so large that the full images could only be seen from above!

Over the next decade, as flight became more common, explorers and scientists were able to view and study the enormous geoglyph images from the sky. Some form geometric figures and patterns. Some are straight lines that run for more than 30 miles (48 km)—the length of nearly 1,000 Olympic swimming pools! And many are in the shape of animals like birds, cats, lizards, and more—some

The Nazca lines depict everything from geometric designs like this spiral (above) to animals like this spider (below).

as large as New York's Empire State Building is tall. But who had carved these mysterious images? And why would they create pictures so enormous you could only see them from the air?

Over the years, scientists came to believe that an ancient Peruvian people known as the Nazca had created the geoglyphs some 1,500 to 2,000 years ago. These people would have hiked up mountains and hilltops to see the impressive images. However, experts aren't sure why the Nazca created them—or even exactly how. Some scientists believe the images were created to scale, meaning the artists would create a small version of the image, and then use math (as well as rope and sticks for guidance) to carve the larger version into the desert floor. Scientists also think that the Nazca possibly created the geoglyphs for religious rituals—some of the straight lines trace the path of the setting sun at certain times of the year.

Today, the mysteries around these large lines have only grown. Scientists using satellites and other technologies have continued to discover more geoglyphs. As they continue to find and study them, experts hope to learn more to put together the pieces of this giant puzzle.

This glyph in Peru may show a large bird known as a condor or a type of long-tailed mockingbird.

Great Geoglyphs

The Nazca in Peru were not the only ones to create geoglyphs. Satellites over India revealed what was a huge asymmetrical spiral that is larger than 38 American football fields. Other giant geoglyphs were found in England, Kazakhstan, the United States, and other places around the globe.

THE LOST CITY OF PETRA

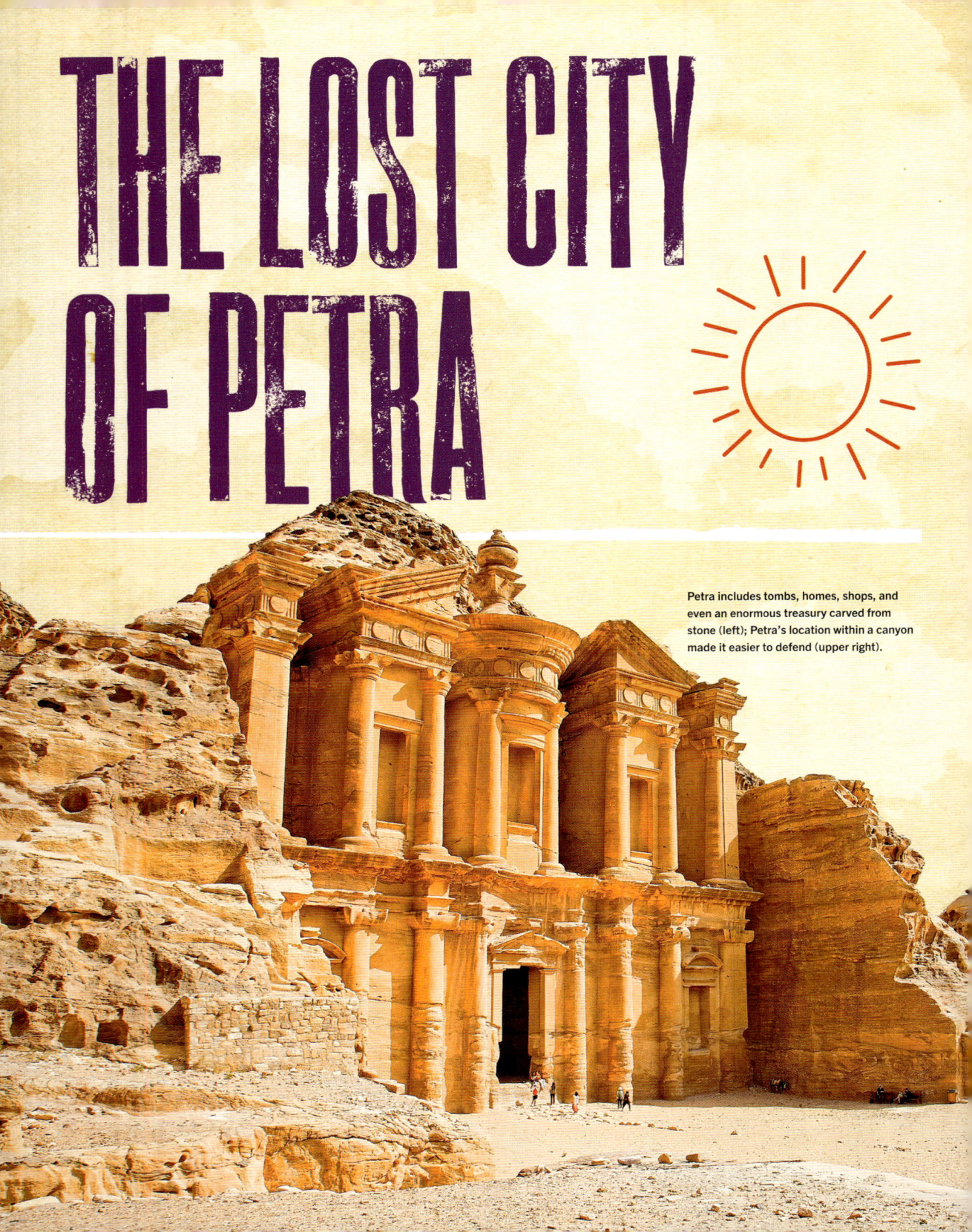

Petra includes tombs, homes, shops, and even an enormous treasury carved from stone (left); Petra's location within a canyon made it easier to defend (upper right).

In 1812, a Swiss explorer named Johann Ludwig Burckhardt was journeying through the desert of Jordan. The land was hot and dry, making for difficult travel, but Burckhardt had a purpose. He had heard stories of a magnificent ruin hidden deep in the desert. Eventually, Burckhardt came upon enormous sandstone hills. He wandered through a winding, narrow canyon, dwarfed on both sides by the pinkish-red rock walls. Eventually, the canyon gave way to a wide-open space and a miraculous sight.

Towering before Burckhardt was a city carved entirely out of rock cliffs. The buildings were massive: Enormous stone pillars and doorways stretched more than six times as tall as an adult human. Over the years, scientists studying this "lost" city—known as Petra—concluded that an ancient civilization called the Nabataeans had built it some 2,400 years ago. The Nabataeans were desert dwellers who made cool, shady homes by carving out shelters in the face of rock cliffs. They had expert ways of transporting, storing, and collecting precious water, and were famous for their wide-ranging trading networks.

Here in Petra, the Nabataeans carved homes, tombs, temples, and even a treasury. However, around the year 551 CE, Petra's inhabitants seem to have mostly abandoned the city. Experts believe that an enormous earthquake drove people away—though the buildings largely survived unscathed. The great desert city remained largely empty for hundreds of years to come. Local and nomadic peoples knew of the city, but purposely avoided it. Eventually, small groups of people began to move back in to the rock city. Today, nearly a million tourists visit Petra every year. But a mystery remains: Why did no one return to the remarkable city for centuries?

Lost Legends

According to local lore, Petra is haunted by powerful spirits known as *djinn*. They are said to reside in large, square funerary monuments known as Djinn Blocks (shown at left) just outside the city. There, they supposedly keep watch over both the living and the dead.

THE CLAY WARRIORS

A HIDDEN ARMY

The day of the discovery began much like any other in 1974. A group of farmers in northwest China was digging a well. As they dug into the soil, they came upon something unusual: shards of ceramic pottery. The workers continued to dig before finding something even stranger: a hidden warrior! However, this was not a real person, but a life-size statue of an ancient Chinese warrior made from a type of clay called terra-cotta.

Stunned by their find, the workers alerted the authorities. Soon, a team of archaeologists arrived. What they found astonished them: Hidden under the earth was an entire army of terra-cotta soldiers—thousands upon thousands of these clay warriors. Amazingly, every soldier was unique, sporting a different hairstyle, pose, or expression. Each one had intricately carved armor, and some led life-size terra-cotta horses or chariots.

Historians soon realized that the soldiers were not there just for show; the terra-cotta army had been positioned to guard a great tomb.

The terra-cotta statues depict warriors with different expressions, hairstyles, and poses.

Archaeologists have discovered more than 8,000 terra-cotta soldiers so far (left);
Some statues were designed to hold weapons or other accessories (middle);
Experts have also uncovered life-size statues of horses (right).

This tomb belonged to Qin Shi Huang, who had declared himself the first emperor of China in 246 BCE when he was just 13 years old. Upon becoming the emperor, Qin immediately began planning for his death and supposed afterlife. He believed that the terra-cotta army would join him in the afterlife as well. He had his burial complex filled with real weapons, as well as countless treasures like precious gems, gold, silver, and jewelry. Today, archaeologists have uncovered more than 8,000 clay soldiers and believe many more have yet to be found.

THE MYSTERIOUS TOMB

What other treasures does the emperor's tomb hold? For now, that remains a mystery because the part of the tomb containing Qin Shi Huang has never been opened! According to historical accounts, the emperor was determined to keep the location of his burial a secret.

Some legends hold that Qin had several thousand of the more than 700,000 workers who built the tomb killed to keep the tomb's location and valuable contents unknown.

Records also claim that Qin ordered his tomb to be filled with complicated—and deadly—booby traps. In addition to its precious treasures, Qin's tomb supposedly contains mechanical crossbows that automatically shoot at intruders, and a river made of poisonous mercury.

However, the tomb really remains sealed because archaeologists are worried about damaging the contents inside. If the tomb *does* contain traps or poisons, they could harm the historical artifacts if set off. And even if the booby traps are just legend, exposing the tomb to open air could cause the ancient items inside to break down or quickly decay. Will we ever know what the mysterious tomb holds? Only time will tell.

LOST TOMBS

Archaeologists, treasure hunters, and historians have long searched for the tombs of famous figures from the past. Some hope to find incredible riches—others are searching for clues that will tell us more about historic events. Dig into more of the most sought-after tombs still lost to history.

CLEOPATRA

The life of the legendary last pharaoh of Egypt has been dramatized in Hollywood films, Shakespearean plays, and countless books. One of the world's most wealthy and powerful rulers, Cleopatra VII was known for her diplomatic alliances. Despite Cleopatra's political savvy, Egypt was no match for Roman conqueror Octavian, who wanted to control Egyptian lands. Cleopatra died in 30 BCE after losing the struggle for power. Legend has it that upon learning she had lost the crucial last battle to control Egypt, Cleopatra allowed herself to be bitten and killed by a venomous snake. To this day, no one has found her final resting place, though many are still looking.

KHUFU

The Great Pyramid of Giza in Egypt is one of the most famous pyramids in the world and also a tomb. It was constructed more than 4,500 years ago in Egypt for the pharaoh Khufu, yet Khufu's body has never been found. Was it looted long ago? Or is there a hidden chamber not yet discovered in the pyramid? Historians hope to find out.

GENGHIS KHAN

The founder of the Mongol Empire in the early 13th century, Genghis Khan ruled the lands from modern-day Ukraine through all of China. His fearsome army conquered and killed millions of people while he was alive. But his exploits didn't stop there. According to legend, everyone who knew about Genghis Khan's tomb—more than 2,000 people—were killed to keep its location secret.

ALEXANDER THE GREAT

He was one of history's most successful military commanders for a reason: More than 2,300 years ago, King Alexander the Great of Macedonia conquered large swaths of lands ranging from what is now Greece to India. After dying of an illness at age 32 in 323 BCE, Alexander was buried in Alexandria, Egypt. However, his tomb was repeatedly ransacked, and the city was damaged by war, earthquakes, and even a tsunami over the years. By the fifth century CE, the tomb's whereabouts had become a mystery, with no clues to its location still today.

BOUDICCA

A Celtic queen in what is now England, Boudicca led a fierce rebellion against the invading Roman Empire in 60 CE. Despite making impressive progress against the much larger Roman army, Boudicca was defeated and killed the following year. The location of her tomb remains unknown, and historians have a list of more than 250 possible places it might be.

CITY BURIED IN TIME

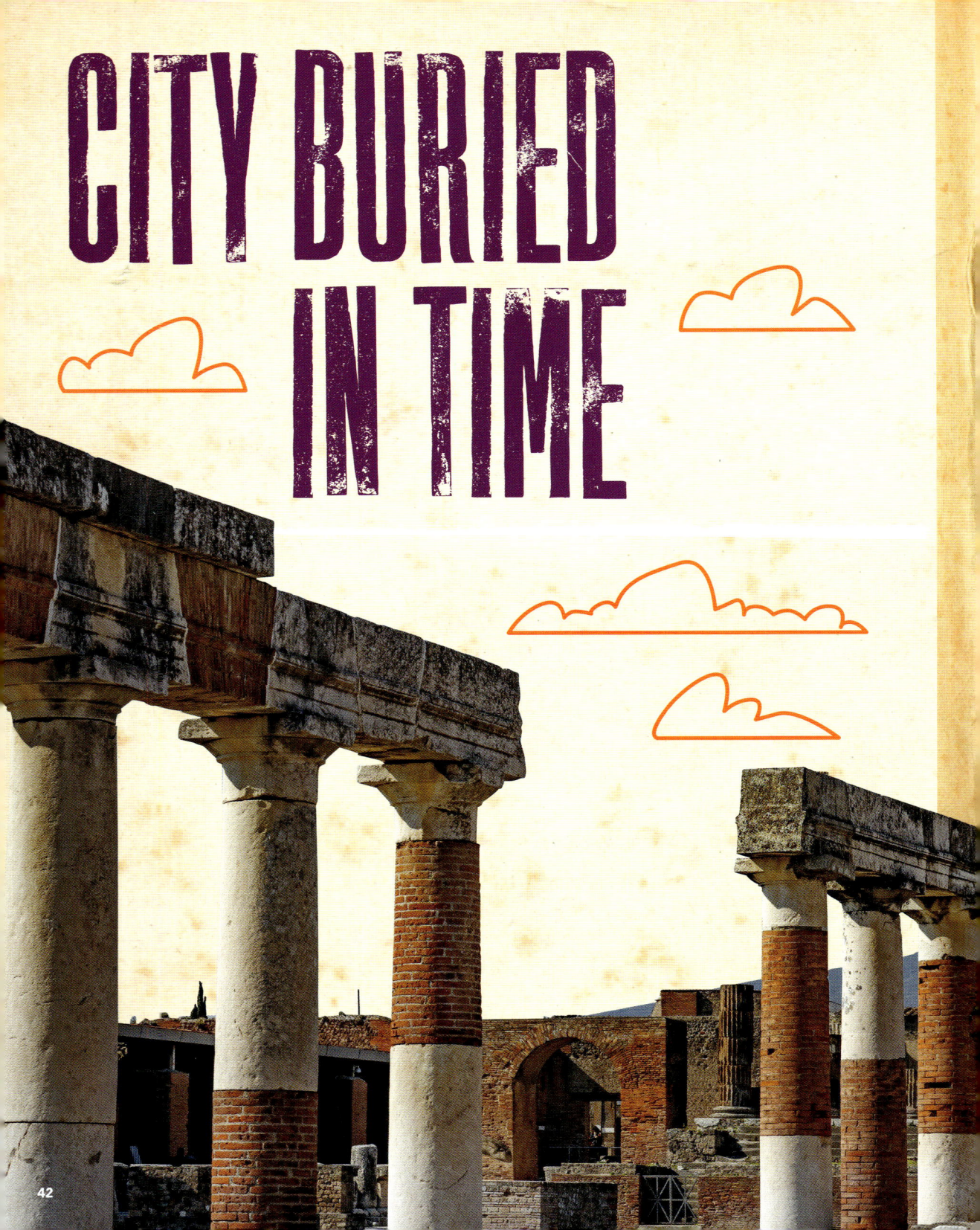

A DEVASTATING ERUPTION

Located at the base of Mount Vesuvius on the coast of the sparkling Mediterranean Sea, Pompeii was a busy resort city where wealthy ancient Roman citizens lived and vacationed. It had elegant homes with courtyards and fountains, bakeries, public squares, shops, and a bustling populace of some 20,000 people. But on August 24 in 79 CE, disaster was about to strike.

That morning, a rumbling earthquake had struck the city. This was nothing new to its residents, who carried on their day as normal once the rolling shocks had subsided. But by noon, a dark cloud had gathered over nearby Mount Vesuvius. This mountain was actually a volcano—and it had just erupted. Thick, burning hot ash fell over the city. Many panicked residents attempted to flee, hurrying to the coast to try to leave by ship as ash and rocks rained over them. Others remained in the city, watching as smoke blocked out the sun entirely and ash continued to fall all around them. The volcanic debris became so heavy that roofs began to collapse. Soon, it had piled up nearly nine feet (2.7 m) high in places—taller than a basketball hoop. It became difficult for people to breathe.

This 19th-century painting depicts Pompeii during Mount Vesuvius's destruction.

43

Near midnight, Mount Vesuvius let out a different kind of eruption (the first of six); a blast of superheated, deadly gases and ash, known as a pyroclastic flow. These flows surged down and around the mountain—including over the city of Pompeii. People had no time to react: Some people lived to tell the tale, but most were consumed by deadly volcanic flows and gases twice as hot as boiling water. As for the city itself, it was buried and lost under the ash.

POMPEII PRESERVED

Following the eruption, Pompeii faded into a distant memory for hundreds of years. In 1592, an Italian architect named Domenico Fontana was overseeing the construction of a canal near Mount Vesuvius. As the team dug, they discovered what appeared to be ancient buildings. No one knew what this site might be, though some suspected it was the lost city of Pompeii. Three centuries later, scientists truly began to dig up the ancient ruins.

Pompeii as it looks today (top left); Casts show Pompeii's victims as they were in their last moments (bottom left).

A wall painting found in the Pompeii archaeological site.

In the 1860s, an archaeologist named Giuseppe Fiorelli led excavations of Pompeii. In addition to the ancient buildings and artifacts preserved in the ash, Fiorelli discovered something shocking: When the citizens of Pompeii died, their bodies had been covered by falling cinders. Over the years, the bodies decayed and disappeared. However, the spaces where the bodies—and their skeletons—had been remained as air pockets in the layers of debris. Fiorelli devised a creative technique to pour plaster into these air pockets. When the plaster dried, it created casts, or statues, made in the shape of the people—and even one guard dog—who had died.

Today, visitors to Pompeii and nearby museums can view the casts of people who once lived in the city. They can also stroll the streets and view preserved artifacts such as clothing, jewels, furniture, art, and even food to imagine what life was once like there. Though the eruption of Mount Vesuvius led to Pompeii's destruction, it also immortalized the city forever, providing historians, scientists, and people today with a glimpse into a real Roman city.

TAKE IT FURTHER

Why do you think people are interested in learning about the past? If you could go back in time, what place and era would you most like to visit?

Today, experts are using lasers to see what was written on these ancient, charred scrolls.

The Lost Library

Pompeii was not the only city that Mount Vesuvius destroyed. Nearby, the homes and citizens of the small town of Herculaneum suffered the same fate. However, there, archaeologists have found something unique: a large library full of ancient Roman scrolls. Though preserved, the scrolls are much too fragile to be opened. So scientists have come up with a unique way to see what information lies in these texts. By using lasers and X-ray technology, they can scan the scrolls and read the secrets they hold.

ANCIENT WORLD WONDERS

Explore the lost ancient wonders of the world—only one of them survives today!

PYRAMIDS OF GIZA

These pyramids in Egypt are the only remaining wonder from the ancient world. Built more than 4,500 years ago as tombs, they would have been covered in sparkling white stone with ornate toppers that were sometimes covered with gold leaf. Over the years, looters spirited away the outer layers, leaving the stone tomb you see today.

STATUE OF ZEUS

Reaching 40 feet (12 m) high, this depiction of the ancient Greek god Zeus gleamed with ivory, ebony, gold, and jewels. It was both a feat of construction and a tremendous display of wealth. The statue originally stood some 2,400 years ago. However, the temple that housed it was ransacked in 426 CE and the precious materials were likely looted.

TEMPLE OF ARTEMIS

This magnificent, colorful temple built in what is now Turkey some 2,500 years ago was dedicated to the ancient Roman goddess Artemis. Made entirely from marble, the temple was renowned for its incredible carvings and sculptures, as well as for the engineering it took to lift each enormous marble block into place. Invading armies destroyed the temple in 262 CE.

MAUSOLEUM AT HALICARNASSUS

Artemisia II, who was the queen of a region in what is now Turkey, ordered this grand mausoleum, or large, aboveground tomb, in honor of her husband, King Mausolus. Historic accounts say that the tomb, which was built more than 2,350 years ago, towered over the land. The mausoleum survived for millennia but began to topple after earthquakes struck the region between the 12th and 15th centuries.

LIGHTHOUSE OF ALEXANDRIA

This giant lighthouse, built around 280 BCE in Alexandria, Egypt, reached more than 350 feet (107 m) high. It was the second-tallest building in the world at the time, after the Pyramids of Giza, and a technological marvel. A fire burned at the top and was reflected by bronze mirrors into a bright beam that guided ships into the port. Earthquakes destroyed the lighthouse by the 14th century.

HANGING GARDENS OF BABYLON

Supposedly built some 2,600 years ago in what is now Iraq, this wonder was said to be a huge, multilevel building with towering gardens of enormous trees and exotic fruits—an incredible feat, considering it was in the middle of a flat, dry grassland! On top of that, the gardens supposedly used spectacular engineering that delivered water against gravity and to the top of the towers. But was it real? See page 140!

COLOSSUS OF RHODES

Some 2,400 years ago, a bronze statue about the size of the Statute of Liberty (without her base) stood at the harbor of the ancient Greek city of Rhodes, located on an island in the Mediterranean. For decades, the statue stood as a testament to the Greek's amazing iron-working skills. However, the statue fell when an earthquake struck around 225 BCE. Its iron scraps remained on Rhodes for centuries, until travelers in the seventh century whisked away the metal to use and sell. Supposedly, it took 900 camels to cart it all away!

CARVED FROM THE CLIFFS

Cliff Palace at Mesa Verde National Park in Colorado, U.S.A. (above); The Long House ruins at Mesa Verde National Park (upper left, opposite).

Though the desert of the American Southwest can be harsh, humans have likely called this region home for some 10,000 years. They developed a civilization that created incredible feats of architecture and engineering, from desert farms to towering cliff palaces.

Around 2,000 years ago, a civilization known as the Ancestral Puebloans emerged in parts of what are now Utah, Arizona, New Mexico, and Colorado. The Ancestral Puebloans created dryland farming techniques that relied on collecting and spreading rainwater and snowmelts to grow squash, corn, and beans. That was far from their greatest achievement. By the 12th century, Ancestral Puebloans had begun to build homes and complexes high on the sides of stone cliffs. They created these impressive complexes using an advanced form of geometry, and by carving directly into the cliffside or by building stone and clay homes called pueblos in high cliff alcoves.

Today's descendants of the Ancestral Puebloans include the Hopi, Zuni, Acoma, and Laguna.

Zuni dancers perform the Eagle Dance.

These incredible complexes—some of which grew into villages of more than 150 rooms—allowed the Ancestral Puebloans to remain safe from attacking enemies. However, by the 14th century, the cliff dwellings were abandoned. Why? Historians aren't sure. Some think that drought may have caused farms to wither. Others think advancing enemies may have driven the Ancestral Puebloans away. Regardless, the dwellings remain magnificent treasure troves of knowledge on how people used mathematics and engineering to master life in the desert long ago. Someday, experts may learn even more—perhaps the answers to the mysteries that remain.

TAKE IT FURTHER

All around the world, humans have learned to live in unusual places. What are some of the ways you can think of that make life easier in tough environments?

Talking Turkey

Today, researchers may be one step closer to discovering what happened to the Ancestral Puebloans—by studying turkey DNA! The Ancestral Puebloans farmed turkeys for food and for their feathers. Scientists comparing DNA from the remains of prehistoric turkeys across the southwestern U.S. discovered matching turkey DNA from the northern Rio Grande area in New Mexico. This suggests that after they abandoned the cliff dwellings, some Ancestral Puebloans may have moved there, bringing their turkeys along too.

GREAT ZIMBABWE

More than 1,000 years ago, a mysterious group of people constructed a great medieval city in what is now Zimbabwe in southern Africa. By the 11th century, the city was thriving. Built atop a hill, the city center included a religious space, an enclosure that may have been a royal residence, and an enormous outer wall. The wall was an incredible feat of engineering: Made without mortar, it relied entirely on stones stacked to fit perfectly together as high as three stories. Outside the large wall, houses across the nearby valley held some 10,000 to 20,000 people.

Who were these people? What was life like in this city—now known as Great Zimbabwe? Historians think the inhabitants were the ancestors of southeastern Africa's Shona people. They likely raised cattle, farmed, and mined gold. Certainly, the city had an extensive trade network; today's ruins contain pottery from ancient China and what is now Iran, as well as coins from the Middle East. Beyond that, experts can't be sure—because the vibrant, wealthy city was mysteriously abandoned in the 15th century.

No one knows what caused the city's inhabitants to leave Great Zimbabwe. Some historians think that the surrounding lands could no longer produce enough food to feed the growing population. What's more, European colonizers who arrived in the 20th century went on to loot and damage the city ruins, meaning that many artifacts and clues to the city's past may have been lost forever.

Various views of Great Zimbabwe (left); Two girls walk by Great Zimbabwe's enormous walls (above).

Lost Civilizations

Great Zimbabwe is far from being the world's only "lost" civilization. Many things might have caused city inhabitants to abandon their home. Food shortages—which may have happened in Great Zimbabwe—and droughts could force people to seek new lands. Approaching invaders could also quickly ruin entire cities, or cause civilizations to flee. Other cities might have encountered tidal waves, drought, earthquakes, volcanic eruptions, or any other number of natural disasters.

Lack of rain, or drought, often makes it impossible for food to grow.

UNEARTHING TENOCHTITLÁN

Mexico City today is a vibrant metropolis of grand boulevards, busy highways, sprawling parks, bustling shops, and many types of homes. But the city also hides a secret beneath its streets: an ancient city once lost.

According to legend, the Aztec—who called themselves the Mexica—spent centuries searching for the perfect place to build their capital. Finally, around 1325, they were traveling through the high mountain plateaus in what is now central Mexico when they came across a sign: an eagle perched atop a cactus clutching a snake in its beak. However, the eagle was on a tiny island in the middle of a large lake. The Aztec did not let this stop them. By building mud islands, they formed a grand city complex right in the middle of Lake Texcoco, complete with wide courtyards, canals, palaces, and temples, including an enormous pyramid known today as the Templo Mayor.

A carved serpent at Templo Mayor, the main temple of Tenochtitlán (above); The unearthed ruins of Templo Mayor in Mexico City (upper right).

By the 16th century, Tenochtitlán, as the city was known, was a thriving hub of some 400,000 people. However, the city met its downfall in 1519, when the Spanish invader Hernán Cortés arrived with an army of conquistadors. These colonizers brought horses, guns, and something far deadlier: a disease known as smallpox, which wiped out many of the Mexica people. By 1521, Cortés had completely conquered Tenochtitlán. Spanish colonizers tore down the temples and grand buildings, using stones to create new cathedrals, churches, and public squares. For centuries, the remains of the Aztec city lay buried. Fortunately, archaeologists have since unearthed many remaining ruins of what was once Tenochtitlán, preserving the city's rich ancient heritage for the future.

TAKE IT FURTHER

What do you think could be hiding right below your feet? A hidden cave, forgotten artifacts, or maybe an entire city? What would you most like to discover?

As many as 200,000 people may have lived at Teotihuacán.

Sacred City

Just outside of Mexico City lies Teotihuacán, a 2,100-year-old ancient complex of paved courtyards, treasure chambers, palaces, and enormous pyramids. Despite these pristine ruins, the city remains something of a mystery: Though the Aztec revered Teotihuacán, they did not build it—and nobody knows for sure who did!

THE MYSTERIES OF THE MOAI

MEET THE MOAI

Carved from volcanic rock and located on the remote island of Rapa Nui (also known as Easter Island), the *moai*, or "Easter Island heads" are grand statues famous for their striking design and huge proportions. They are also known for an enduring mystery: How exactly did people manage to create—and erect—these huge figures using only ancient technologies?

More than 1,000 years ago, Polynesian sailors arrived at an island located some 2,200 miles (1,900 km) off the coast of Chile. They named the island after themselves: Rapa Nui. There, they settled and created a civilization based on farming and fishing. By the 13th century, the Rapa Nui began making the humanlike statues known as moai. Made of volcanic stone, these enormous statues feature striking, stylized faces atop long bodies. Many sit on shrine bases, known as *ahu*. Some sport stone headdresses called *pukao*. Historians think that the Rapa Nui may have carved the moai to represent their ancestors or to honor chiefs and leaders. The pukao might have symbolized hairstyles or hats.

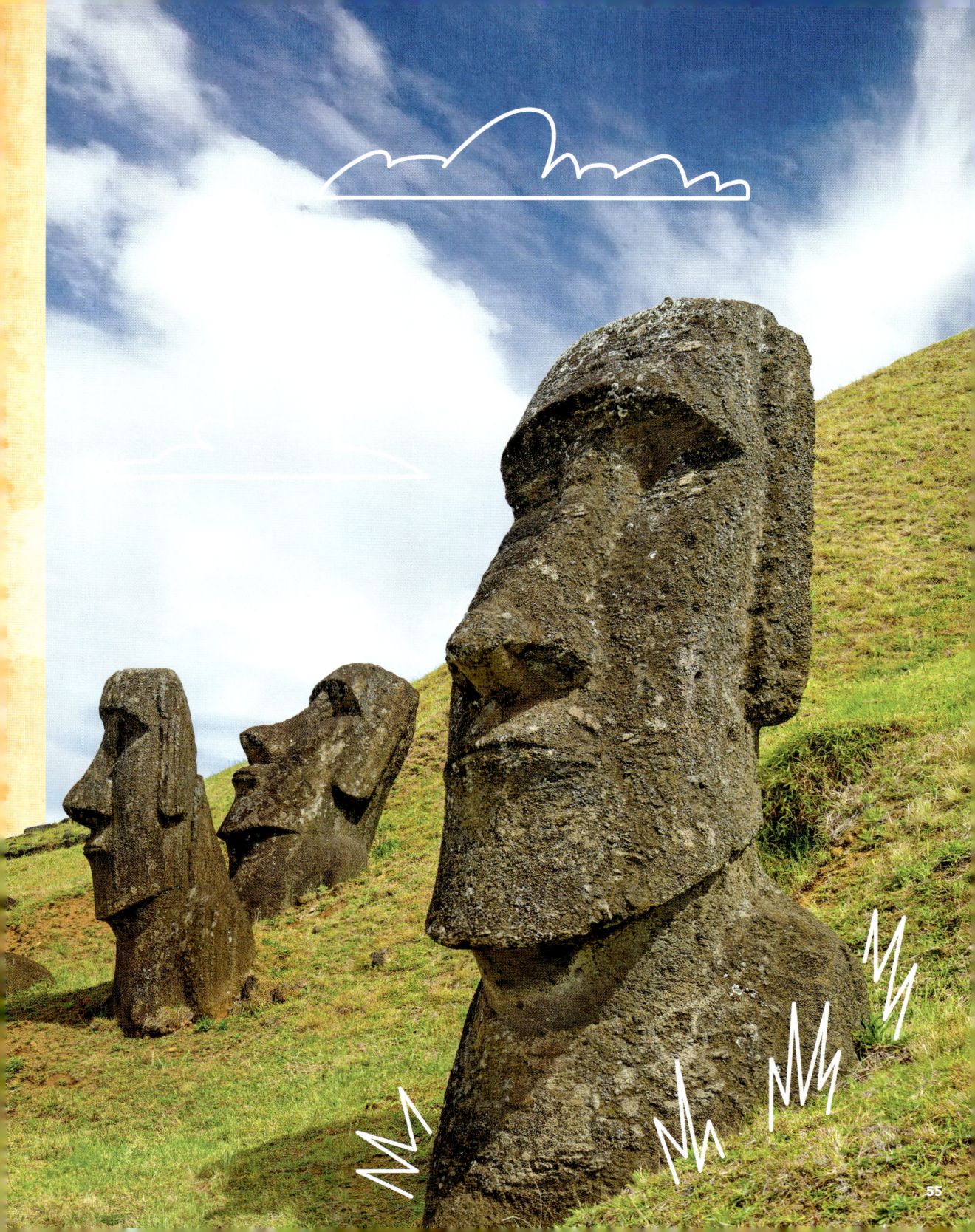

To carve these figures, the Rapa Nui used stone picks to shape volcanic rocks. Next came the baffling part: After carving them, the sculptors managed to erect these giant statues upright atop their ahu. Even today, this would be no easy feat. The height of the tallest upright moai is 32.8 feet (10 m), or the height of a three-story building! The largest moai ever created—an unfinished statue known as El Gigante—was even bigger, stretching for 72 feet (22 m), or about seven stories. In modern times, workers would rely on cranes or other machines to lift and erect statues that large. But centuries ago, the Rapa Nui did not have access to these things. Even so, they managed to move and lift the moai—and scientists aren't sure how!

MOVING THE MOAI

Although experts don't know how the Rapa Nui erected the moai, they have some ideas. Some historians believe that the Rapa Nui probably moved the giant statues using a combination of wooden logs, wooden sledges, and ropes. To do this, the Rapa Nui may have rolled the large statues over a collection of logs, or pulled them on sledges. Then, they would have secured the moai's base before using long ropes to pull the statue upright. However, other experts think that builders may have "walked" the moai to their destinations using a lasso-like rope technique. To figure out the most likely solution, many historians have even conducted experiments where they attempted to move moai reproductions using possible ancient techniques.

THE FATE OF THE RAPA NUI

On top of how the Rapa Nui transported the moai, another mystery remains: What happened to the Rapa Nui themselves? By the late 19th century, the population of Rapa Nui—which once numbered as many as 9,000—had dwindled to the hundreds. Some historians believe many Rapa Nui were

FUN FACT

El Gigante—the largest moai ever carved but never erected—weighs almost 200 tons (181 t)—more than two 737 passenger airplanes!

forced to abandon the island sometime before the arrival of European explorers in the early 1700s. According to one theory, the inhabitants of Rapa Nui cut down too many trees, making it so that the island could no longer support them. But other historians think that the civilization of Rapa Nui flourished until the arrival of Europeans. They believe the civilization collapsed when European explorers introduced new diseases and invaders kidnapped or enslaved the Rapa Nui.

TAKE IT FURTHER

Around the world, humans go to great efforts to create incredible buildings, works of art, and monuments. If you could build a monument, what would it be and what would it represent?

New Names

Today, the moai are often known as the "Easter Island heads." This is partly because the first European explorer to reach Rapa Nui arrived on Easter Sunday, 1722. On top of that, early visitors didn't realize that the statues were more than just heads. Over the centuries, dirt had built up to bury the statues' bodies—making them look like giant carved heads.

MORE COLOSSAL CREATIONS

For hundreds—and even thousands—of years, humans have been creating larger-than-life constructions and statues (known as megalithic structures) without the help of modern technology.

GGANTIJA

Ġgantija of Malta's Gozo Island may be one of the oldest megalithic structures in the world. First built more than 5,500 years ago, the temple complex includes enormous stone walls, many of which were once painted red. The temples, which also included statues and places for fires, served as a center for ceremonial rites and rituals.

PLAIN OF JARS

Located in Laos, the Plain of Jars is what it sounds like: a field filled with enormous stone jars, some nearly twice the height of an adult human. Archaeologists believe the jars, which may be up to 3,000 years old, may have been used as burial grounds for ancient humans. Legends, however, hold that giants used the jars as drinking cups. Cheers!

STONEHENGE

Built some 4,500 years ago in England, Stonehenge is one of the most famous prehistoric monuments in the world. Historians do not know who created the circles of massive standing stones, but think it may have served as a temple, burial monument, or way of studying the skies.

DOLMEN DE BAGNEUX

Historians aren't sure exactly how Europe's ancient dolmens, or tombs, were erected—like the one built in France some 5,000 years ago by an unknown group of people. After all, the stones of the tomb weigh an estimated 500 tons (454 t)—or more than 70 large African elephants. But experts think that the construction may have involved piling dirt around the tomb's sides to slide the enormous roof on top.

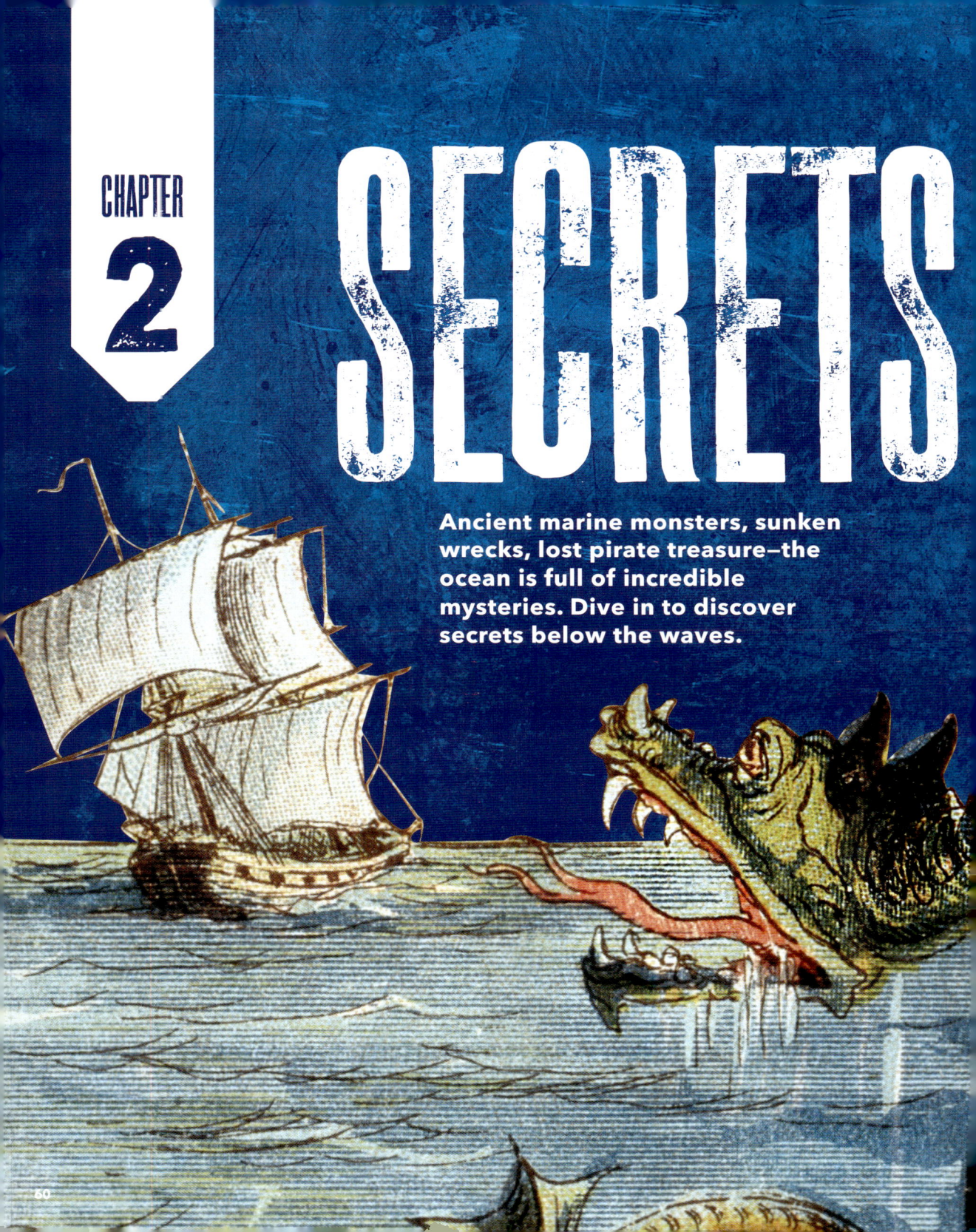

CHAPTER 2

SECRETS

Ancient marine monsters, sunken wrecks, lost pirate treasure—the ocean is full of incredible mysteries. Dive in to discover secrets below the waves.

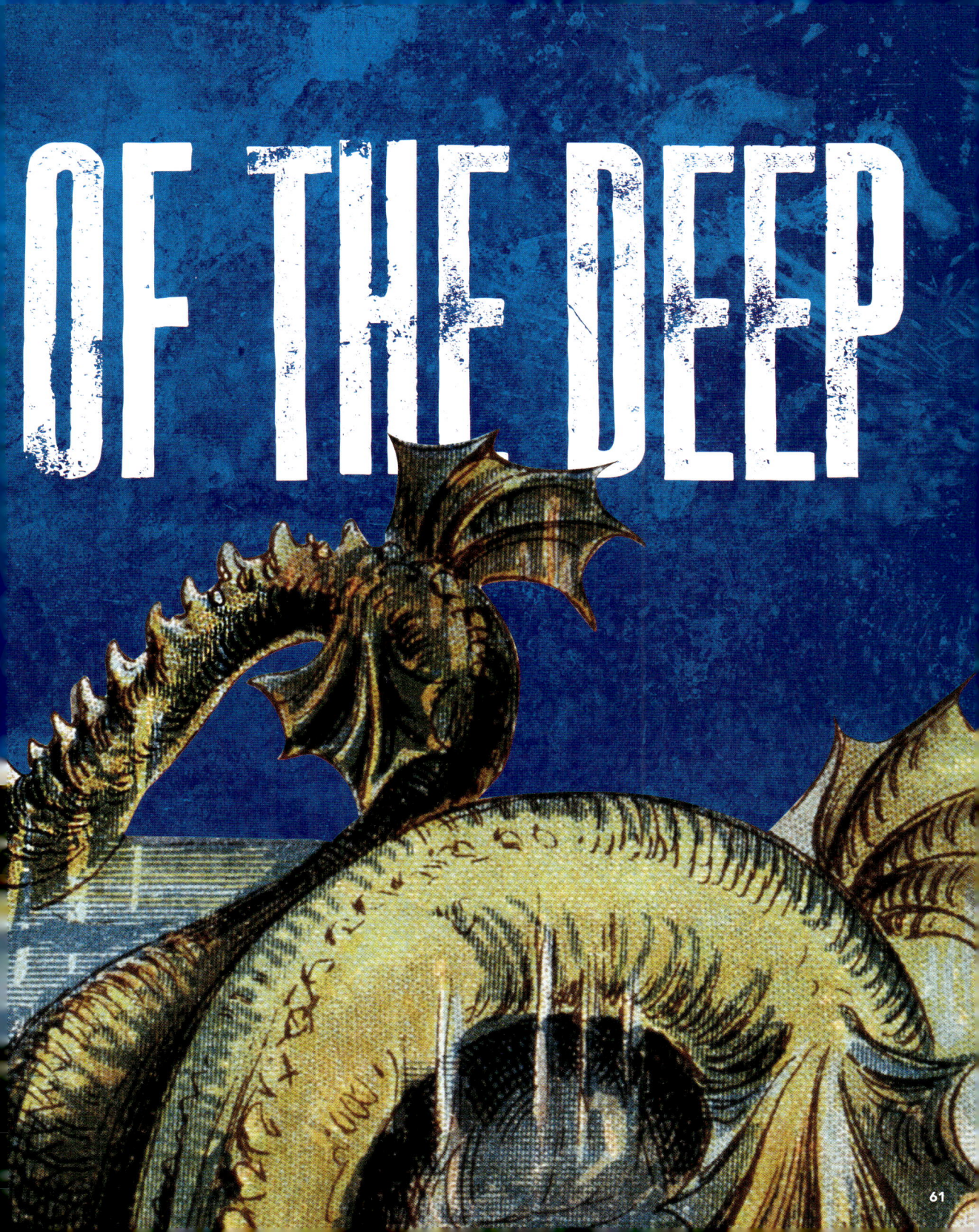

OF THE DEEP

ANCIENT MARINE MONSTERS

MASSIVE MEGALODON

Among the top predators of the ocean, today's great white sharks can reach lengths of up to 20 feet (6 m), or more than three times the length of an adult human. But that's nothing compared to the ancient *Carcharocles megalodon*, or *megalodon*. These fearsome sharks, which lived between 3 and 17 million years ago, could reach up to 60 feet (18 m) long—that's three times the size of the largest great white shark today. In fact, a *megalodon* could have swallowed a great white whole!

Thousands of years ago, gigantic and powerful creatures ruled the waters. Those creatures have since been lost to time—at least, until scientists were able to discover fantastic fossils and other traces of the fierce beasts that once terrorized the seas.

SWIMMING SCORPION

Had humans lived 450 to 200 million years ago, they likely would have come face-to-face with **eurypterids**, enormous marine scorpions that swam in both the salty seas and bodies of fresh water. The largest eurypterid could grow longer than an adult human—at about 8 feet (2.5 m)—and snatched prey using its strong pincers.

INFAMOUS PLESIOSAURUS

Perhaps the most famous of all prehistoric marine reptiles, **Plesiosaurus** is known for its long neck, wide body, and paddle-like flippers. This marine monster used its needle-sharp teeth to snag unsuspecting fish. The largest *Plesiosaurus* stretched about 50 feet (15 m) long.

MEGA MOSASAURUS

Some 66 to 99 million years ago, **Mosasaurus hoffmanni** ruled the ocean. This marine reptile had a large head with a strong snout and sharp teeth, a long, serpentlike body, and a mighty tail and flippers. The largest could reach lengths of 56 feet (17 m). Scientists think that the *Mosasaurus* may have rammed prey to death using its snout, or may have produced venom.

KING CROCODILIAN

Millions of years ago, monsters didn't just swim the seas; they lurked in rivers too. This enormous crocodilian, **Sarcosuchus imperator**, lived around 110 million years ago. About as long as a school bus, the crocodilian's head alone was the size of an adult human. *Sarcosuchus imperator* likely hid at the edges of African rivers to snatch—and eat!—dinosaurs.

THE LOST CAVE

In 2007, divers were exploring and mapping an underwater cave system in Quintana Roo, Mexico. This was dangerous work; divers could easily get lost in the dark, twisting tunnels. But then, they came across something amazing: Bones were littered across the cave floors. And not just any bones, but the ancient fossils of prehistoric animals.

Some 38,000 years ago, Earth was experiencing an Ice Age. Much of the planet's water was frozen in great ice sheets, meaning that water levels were lower. This cave, now known as Hoyo Negro, was not underwater at the time. Unfortunately for the Ice Age animals, the cave was still dangerous, and many died inside. However, this was good for later archaeologists. As temperatures across the planet warmed over the millennia, ice melted and water levels rose. Hoyo Negro filled with water, preserving a lost world for later generations to study.

But the cave wasn't just home to animal bones. Scientists also found a fossil of a teenage girl who died some 12,000 to 13,000 years ago. This girl, now known as Naia, helped archaeologists uncover more incredible secrets from the past. By studying Naia's DNA, archaeologists discovered that Naia likely descended from an ancient group of people living in Asia. This discovery helped confirm the theory that ancient humans migrated into the Americas from Asia more than 15,000 years ago.

Into the Americas

Most scientists think that humans first arrived in the Americas at least 15,000 years ago. To get there, they may have crossed a piece of land now known as Beringia. Today, Beringia, which connects Asia to North America, is underwater. But during the Ice Age, Beringia appeared as dry land. Over thousands of years, humans may have traveled over this land, possibly following moving herds of animals. And for thousands of years after that, they likely spread through the Americas.

Beringia

POLYNESIAN WAYFINDING

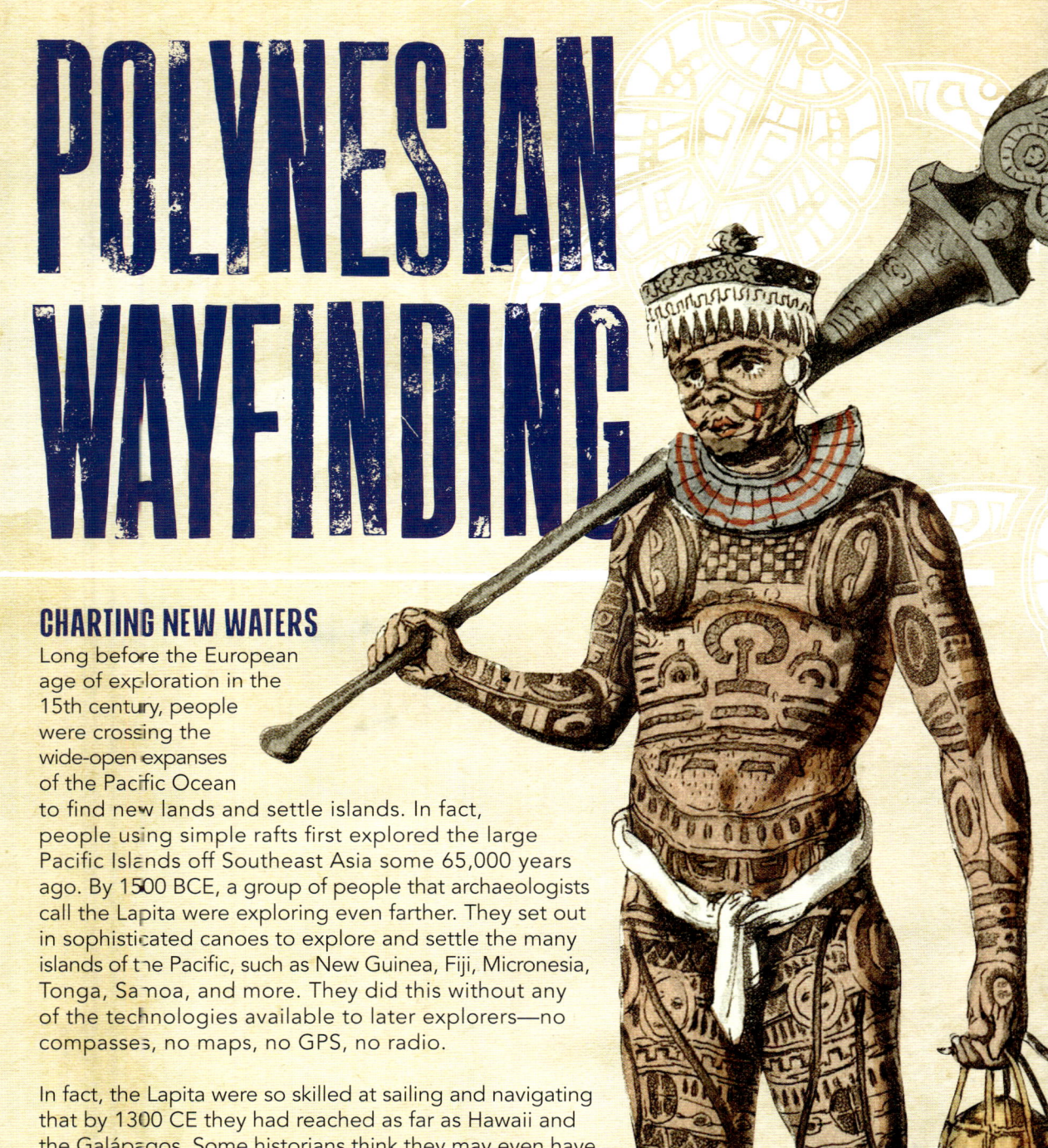

CHARTING NEW WATERS

Long before the European age of exploration in the 15th century, people were crossing the wide-open expanses of the Pacific Ocean to find new lands and settle islands. In fact, people using simple rafts first explored the large Pacific Islands off Southeast Asia some 65,000 years ago. By 1500 BCE, a group of people that archaeologists call the Lapita were exploring even farther. They set out in sophisticated canoes to explore and settle the many islands of the Pacific, such as New Guinea, Fiji, Micronesia, Tonga, Samoa, and more. They did this without any of the technologies available to later explorers—no compasses, no maps, no GPS, no radio.

In fact, the Lapita were so skilled at sailing and navigating that by 1300 CE they had reached as far as Hawaii and the Galápagos. Some historians think they may even have sailed all the way to the Americas and back, centuries before European explorers ever reached the continents! Over time, these Lapita settlements grew into different

Since ancient Lapita times, the sea turtle has symbolized seafaring and navigation in many Polynesian cultures.

19th-century drawing by a British artist of a man from the Pacific Islands (left); A modern re-creation of a traditional Pacific Islander ship (below).

HINEMOANA

ocean-based societies, today collectively known as the many Pacific Islander cultures. But how, exactly, did the Lapita and their descendants explore the vast Pacific? What skills did they use?

This long-standing art of ocean navigation is known as wayfinding. Wayfinders can figure out their direction by memorizing the positions of hundreds of stars, examining the locations of the sun and moon, or analyzing shadows the sun casts. These navigators can "read" swells, temperatures, and ocean currents. They know how to search for land by looking at the colors, shapes, and movements of clouds, or by understanding patterns of bird flight to follow flocks to dry shores.

Wayfinders use weather patterns, stars, water temperature, and more to navigate.

A LOST (AND FOUND) TRADITION

For centuries, wayfinding remained a mystery to outsiders. When Europeans first came into contact with Pacific Island cultures—often through brutal violence and colonization—their racist beliefs led them to make incorrect assumptions. For example, many European explorers refused to believe that the Pacific Islanders had mastered ocean navigation without any modern technology used in other parts of the world. Over time, knowledge of how people had come to the Pacific Islands began to disappear because it was often passed in the form of oral tradition, or shared stories, songs, poems, and more. But as colonizers settled the area, they discouraged, banned, and even punished many of the Pacific Islander traditions.

Because of this, wayfinding seemed to be a lost art by the 1950s. However, in the 1970s, a group of scientists, artists, and surfers created the Polynesian Voyaging Society to better understand the history of wayfinding. In 1976, a Pacific Islander from Micronesia named Pius "Mau" Piailug led the Polynesian Voyaging Society on a voyage from Hawaii to Tahiti using wayfinding techniques. Mau and the society went on to train new crew members and sailors in the art of wayfinding, ensuring that the skill would never be lost.

On top of that, breakthroughs in DNA studies, computer models, and other scientific technologies allowed scientists to trace the ancient settlement of the Pacific Islands, confirming once and for all that Pacific Islander oral histories were correct.

TAKE IT FURTHER

Throughout history, humans have explored the far reaches of the world—and even into space! Why do you think humans explore? Where would you most like to explore?

One More Mystery

More than 3,500 years ago, the Lapita and their descendants explored vast regions of the Pacific. But around 1000 BCE, exploration and settling suddenly stopped. This "long pause," as it is known, lasted for about 1,000 years. But scientists and historians don't really know what caused it. Some think that a large change in the weather or ocean may have occurred—such as a long season of violent storms, or unusual wind patterns.

WHO WERE THE SEA PEOPLES?

An engraving depicts Pharaoh Ramesses III defending against the Sea Peoples some 3,100 years ago.

For much of the Bronze Age (about 3000 to 1200 BCE), societies around the Mediterranean and the Near East flourished. Though small by today's standards, these civilizations—from the ancient Egyptians to the Minoans in modern-day Crete to the Babylonians in what is now Iraq, Syria, and Iran—celebrated rich cultures, widespread trade, and artistic and architectural marvels. But starting in 1177 BCE, almost all the societies of the Bronze Age began to collapse, leaving behind a struggling dark age. What happened? The only people left to tell the tale were the survivors: the ancient Egyptians.

According to Egyptian King Ramses II, waves of mysterious marauders had suddenly invaded the lands, bringing destruction and ruin to formerly mighty kingdoms: "They came boldly sailing in their warships from the midst of the sea, and none could withstand them." These Sea Peoples, as they later became known, arrived from the ocean and laid waste to civilizations in parts of Africa, Europe, and Asia. In fact, the only people known to defend themselves successfully against the mysterious Sea Peoples were the ancient Egyptians, who used a combination of archers to rain down arrows on the enemy, and grappling hooks to pull their ships to shore where more Egyptian soldiers attacked them.

Almost as quickly as they came, the Sea Peoples disappeared. To this day, historians have no consensus on where the attackers came from, where they returned, or even why they struck. Based on the varying descriptions in ancient Egyptian accounts, some scholars believe that the Sea Peoples may not have been one culture, but a cooperating group of members from many civilizations. Others contend that the Sea Peoples were refugees fleeing their homelands and searching for a new place to settle. Regardless, almost everything about them remains a mystery to this day.

An illustration of a battle between the Sea Peoples and King Ramses III and his soldiers.

THE SUNKEN CITY

Today, Egypt's Alexandria is a modern city filled with cars, businesses, a thriving port, and loads of tourists. But just off its shores lies another, far older Alexandria. Founded by Alexander the Great (see p. 41) in 332 BCE, the original Alexandria was also a sight to be seen. The city was a treasure trove of palaces, temples, and even the famed Library of Alexandria. It was also later the home of Cleopatra VII (see p. 40), the Lighthouse of Alexandria (see p. 47), and engineering marvels such as one of the world's first coin-operated vending machines.

Thanks to earthquakes and tsunamis, much of ancient Alexandria ended up underwater (above); Archaeologists have discovered many ancient statues, such as these three (at right) that were brought up from the ocean floor in 2001 and this one of a sphinx (top right).

In 365 CE, tragedy struck: An enormous tsunami swept over the city and surrounding areas, killing many thousands of people. Over the next few centuries, additional earthquakes caused some of the magnificent city to slowly slide into the sea. For centuries, sunken treasures remained seemingly lost forever—or, at least, until the 1990s. French archaeologist Jean-Yves Empereur and Egyptian cinematographer Asma el-Bakri were swimming in the waters off modern Alexandria in an area that the Egyptian military had previously marked as off-limits. The pair was stunned by what they saw: enormous stone statues, ancient columns, and more. However, the site was in danger: Local construction meant that new concrete would crush these priceless artifacts.

Luckily, Empereur and el-Bakri successfully petitioned the Egyptian government to halt construction, allowing archaeologists to explore the watery depths. There, experts have uncovered barnacle-crusted statues, stone sphinxes, golden treasures, and possibly even the ruins of Cleopatra's palace. They have also discovered parts of the Lighthouse of Alexandria, including sections of its enormous door. Today, advancements in underwater archaeology have even allowed divers to map out the original harbor of Alexandria—but mysteries still remain. Scientists hope to one day discover Alexander the Great's tomb, or remnants of the city's famed library.

Lost Knowledge

Founded sometime around 295 BCE, the Library of Alexandria held one of the largest book and record collections of the ancient world. However, many of the tomes were lost in 48 BCE when warring Roman armies accidentally set it ablaze (depicted at right in a 19th-century illustration). Then, in the fourth century, Christian mobs swept through Alexandria, intent on destroying anything—including books—they viewed as contrary to their beliefs. They sacked the rebuilt library, bringing its days to an end.

UNDERWATER CITIES AROUND THE WORLD

Dive deep to see submerged cities around the globe.

DOGGERLAND

Some 50,000 years ago, the United Kingdom was not a group of islands, but a peninsula connected to mainland Europe by a stretch of land. For thousands of years, people lived in this region, known as Doggerland. However, a series of tsunamis around 8,200 years ago submerged the land—and its inhabitants—in the ocean.

LAKE TITICACA

Bolivia's Lake Titicaca houses a secret—or rather, several secrets. At the lake's bottom lie some 25 underwater sites containing artifacts belonging to the Inca and Tiwanaku civilizations. Experts have found some 20,000 artifacts, including gold, stone monuments, jewels, and objects that are nearly 1,000 years old.

PORT ROYAL

During the golden age of piracy, Port Royal, Jamaica, was a hub of illegal activities, pirate dens, and executions. That is, until 1692, when an enormous earthquake and a subsequent tsunami caused it to sink into the sea.

SHICHENG

A stunning, 16th-century city, Shicheng, China (also known as Lion City), featured carved stone buildings as well as statues of lions, phoenixes, and dragons. In 1959, the Chinese government relocated the city's residents to make way for a dam, sinking the city in the newly created Qiandao Lake. Recently, divers have begun to excavate the once lost city.

BLACKBEARD'S TREASURE

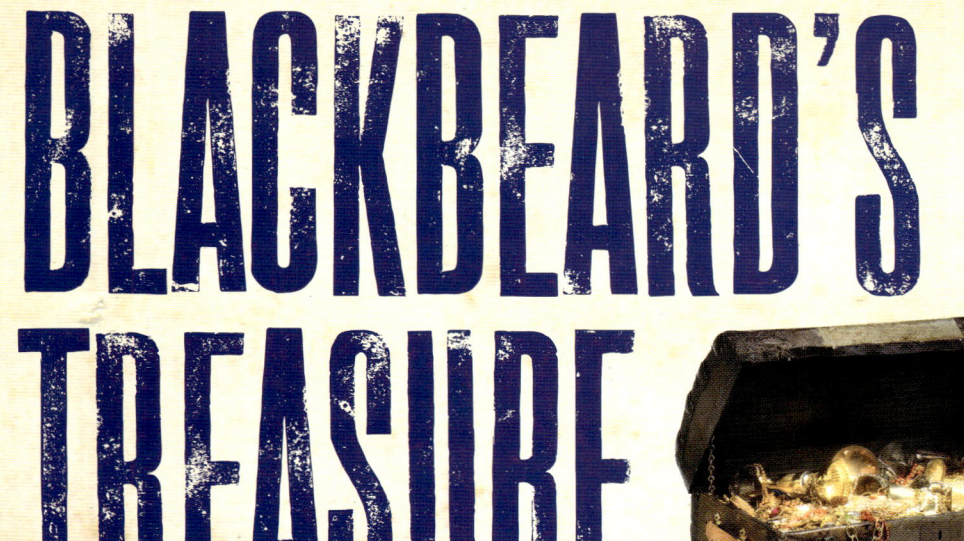

A DREADED PIRATE

At the start of the 18th century, rumors spread of a new pirate captain terrorizing the seas. This man was said to be terrifyingly cruel. According to legend, he could shoot two pistols at once and would murder one of his own crew as easily as he would an enemy.

This man was Blackbeard. Though historians aren't sure which rumors were true and which were exaggerated, Blackbeard was most definitely a notorious pirate captain. He was famous for commanding four ships to seize treasure up and down the Atlantic, ruthlessly terrorizing the sailors of captive vessels. Even more frightening, he was famed for setting lit matches in his long, tangled, black beard to make it appear to smoke all on its own, as if he weren't quite human.

Blackbeard ruled the seas for several years, supposedly amassing an enormous haul of gold, jewels, and silks. But by 1718, the British Navy had had enough. Earlier that year, Blackbeard had run aground on shallow waters off North Carolina's Ocracoke Island. Though Blackbeard and his crew escaped unharmed, his ship, the *Queen Anne's Revenge*, sank beneath the seas. The British Navy arrived in

Experts examine a cannon recovered from Blackbeard's ship.

the region not long after. They surrounded Blackbeard on the island where a fierce battle took place and killed the fearsome pirate. His rule had finally ended.

HIDDEN TREASURE?

For nearly three centuries, only legends of Blackbeard remained. Then, in 1996, a private team was exploring the seafloor off North Carolina when they came across something unexpected: a shipwreck. This wreck appeared to be quite old. It was packed with lead cannons, cannonballs, and other artifacts dating to the early 1700s. Soon, an archaeological team confirmed that this was, in fact, *Queen Anne's Revenge*—legendary Blackbeard's very ship. However, experts soon noticed that something appeared to be missing from the ship: treasure.

Make no mistake: The wreck of *Queen Anne's Revenge* was an invaluable treasure all on its own. But Blackbeard was famous for raiding merchant ships and seizing priceless valuables. So where could those goods be? Some experts speculate that the sinking of *Queen Anne's Revenge* might have been part of Blackbeard's plan all along; perhaps the captain hoped to hide his treasure for himself, claiming it had gone down with the ship. Whether or not he intended the sinking, most historians agree that Blackbeard had plenty of time to spirit away any treasure, and perhaps even stash it in a safe hiding place on Ocracoke Island.

TAKE IT FURTHER

Why would reputation be important to a pirate? How might pirates make themselves seem scarier than they actually were?

The Truth of the Terror

With his bloodthirsty reputation, Blackbeard was—and still is—infamous. Despite the stories, one of the biggest mysteries surrounding Blackbeard doesn't even involve lost treasure, gruesome murders, or ghastly ghosts. Instead, the mystery is Blackbeard himself: Historians still don't know the pirate's true identity. Many historians believe that Blackbeard went by the name Edward Teach and may have been a wealthy ship captain's son who left a life in the navy to become a dreaded pirate captain. However, other experts think this may have been a fake name, meaning Blackbeard's life is still a mystery. (This illustration is based on an 18th-century engraving by the artist B. Cole.)

"X" MARKS THE SPOT

It's a familiar story: Fearsome pirates haul their loot to a deserted island, then bury chests gleaming with gold and jewels deep in the sand. The only trace is a map that marks the treasure's location with a giant "X." According to scholars, however, real pirates rarely buried their treasure. For one thing, "treasure" to a pirate could mean anything valuable—that included expensive spices, sugar, and silks, all of which would go bad if buried. For another, pirates usually wanted to spend their loot as quickly as they could!

But it's not all fiction: The legend of buried treasure may have come from one famous pirate who really did stash his loot in a hidden location. That pirate was William Kidd, a fierce British pirate who terrorized the Atlantic in the 17th century. Captain Kidd, as he was known, may have started as a privateer, a pirate officially employed by the government and instructed to raid ships of enemy countries. Authorities expected privateers to share their loot with the government. But after getting a taste for treasure, Kidd may have struck out on his own as a pirate. Some scholars think the truth was more complicated, and that the British government betrayed Kidd during a time of changing attitudes toward privateers.

Either way, Kidd caught wind that the authorities were seeking him. According to legend, Kidd stopped at least once to hide his treasure and actions from authorities. Unfortunately for him, this was not enough; British officials executed Captain Kidd in 1701. However, they never found his treasure. Most tales report that Kidd buried gold valued at a million dollars in today's money on Gardiners Island, off Long Island, New York. But more of Kidd's treasure may be scattered around the world. In 2015, archaeologists found a 121-pound (55-kg) silver bar off Madagascar that they believe, thanks to markings on the bar, was part of Kidd's haul.

Many tales and illustrations described Captain Kidd as a fearsom pirate (left); A map (top right) and illustration (bottom right) from a 1915 copy of Treasure Island, a tale that popularized the idea of pirates burying their treasure.

Making Treasure Maps

Although Captain Kidd's life as a pirate did not end successfully, his legend lived on. Kidd's tale helped inspire Edgar Allen Poe to write a short story about treasure, "The Gold Bug," in 1843. The novelist Robert Louis Stevenson wrote the Kidd-inspired novel, *Treasure Island*, in 1883. These two stories helped popularize the concept of treasure maps and buried pirate booty for readers in Britain and the United States.

PIRATE QUEEN

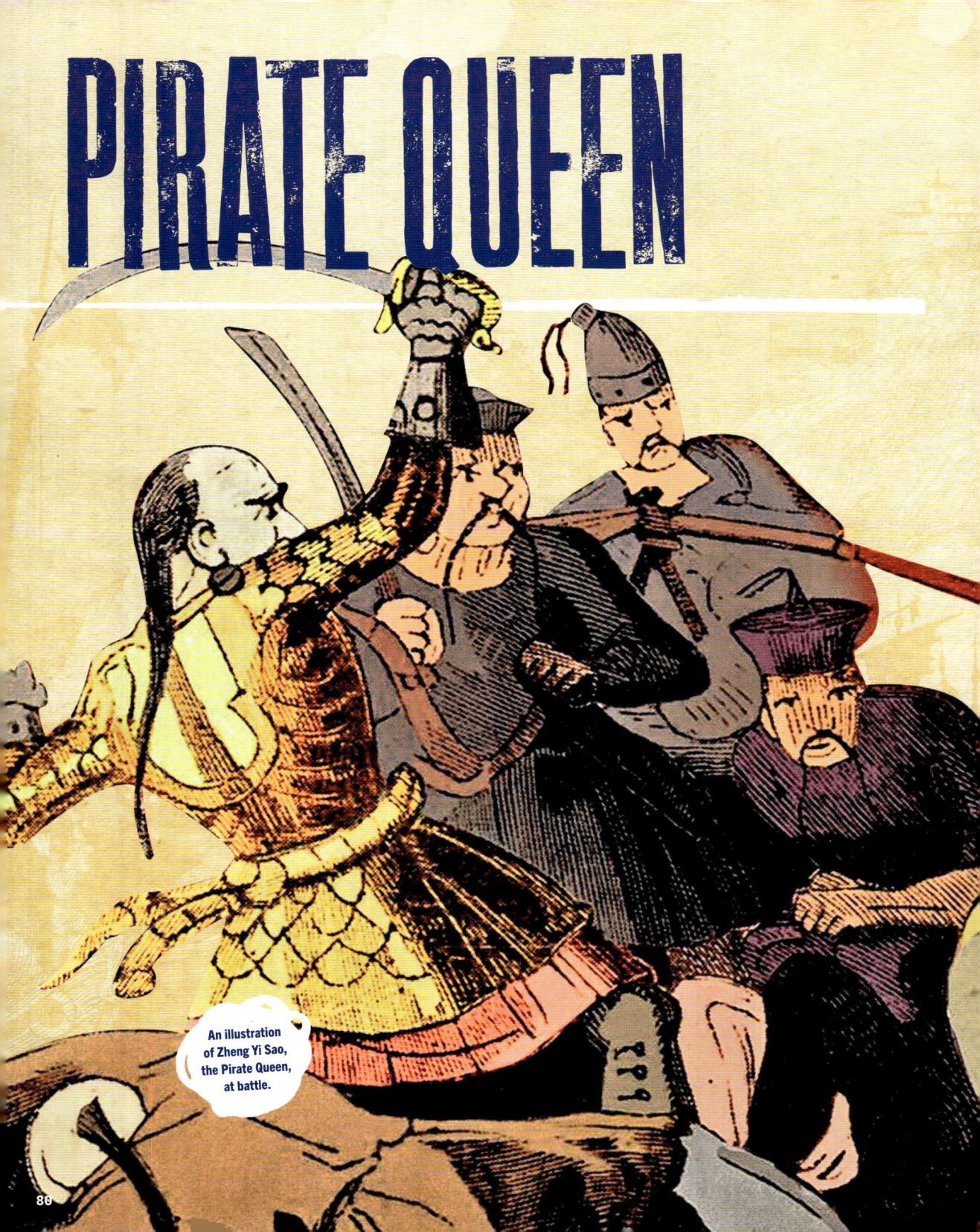

An illustration of Zheng Yi Sao, the Pirate Queen, at battle.

TAKE IT FURTHER

What do you think made Zheng so successful? How was Zheng different from other pirates you've read about?

Think of the most famous pirates you can: Who comes to mind? For many people, the image of a pirate goes hand in hand with a bearded, swashbuckling man sailing the Caribbean Sea. But history's most successful and legendary pirate was a Chinese woman named Zheng Yi Sao (also often known as Ching Shih).

Born in southern China around 1775, Zheng grew up working on boats. There, she met and married a pirate named Zheng Yi. Together, the couple created an impressive pirate super-squad. They brought together several different groups of raiders to unite under their leadership. Altogether, their pirate fleet included more than 40,000 sailors and 600 ships. When Zheng Yi died suddenly in 1807, Zheng took sole command.

After taking charge, Zheng grew her pirate fleet to more than 70,000 sailors and 1,200 ships—more than 100 times the number of crewmen that served under the famed Blackbeard (see p. 76). Her power grew, too, and soon she ruled the South China Sea. In fact, Zheng governed her fleet as more of a queen than a captain. She instituted strict behavior laws and rules for the pirates. She also kept a communal treasury, sort of like a shared bank, that served the whole fleet.

By 1810, Zheng had become so powerful that the Chinese government sought help from other countries to end Zheng's reign. Rather than continue to battle, Zheng successfully negotiated a brilliant surrender that allowed her sailors to keep their treasure, avoid jail, and even join the Chinese Navy. Zheng herself retired and went on to live a quiet life, while leaving behind an impressive legacy.

LOST LEGENDS

QUEEN TEUTA

More than 2,200 years ago, this queen of Illyria (in what is now Albania) commanded her own navy. Teuta led her sailors against nearby enemy kingdoms, including Greece and Rome.

FRANCIS DRAKE

Today, Sir Francis Drake is best remembered for his life as an explorer whose voyages led to the colonization of North America. However, he was also an English privateer who terrorized and captured countless Spanish ships in the 16th century.

SAYYIDA AL HURRA

In the 16th century, Sayyida al Hurra was both the queen of Tétouan, Morocco, and a renowned pirate. She became famous not for her raiding, but for her skills of diplomacy and forming alliances.

BLACK CAESAR

According to legend, Black Caesar was an African chieftain who was abducted and forced into slavery. However, he escaped, and after serving on Blackbeard's crew in the 18th century, went on to captain his own ship, supposedly stashing his loot in southeastern Florida.

ANNE BONNY AND MARY READ

In the 18th century, Anne Bonny (left) took to the sea to join the pirate crew of the infamous Jack Rackham, or Calico Jack. During this time, she met Mary Read (right), who, according to legend, sneaked aboard while disguised as a man. Together, the pair earned a reputation for their fierce fighting skills and bravery.

THE MYSTERY OF THE MARY CELESTE

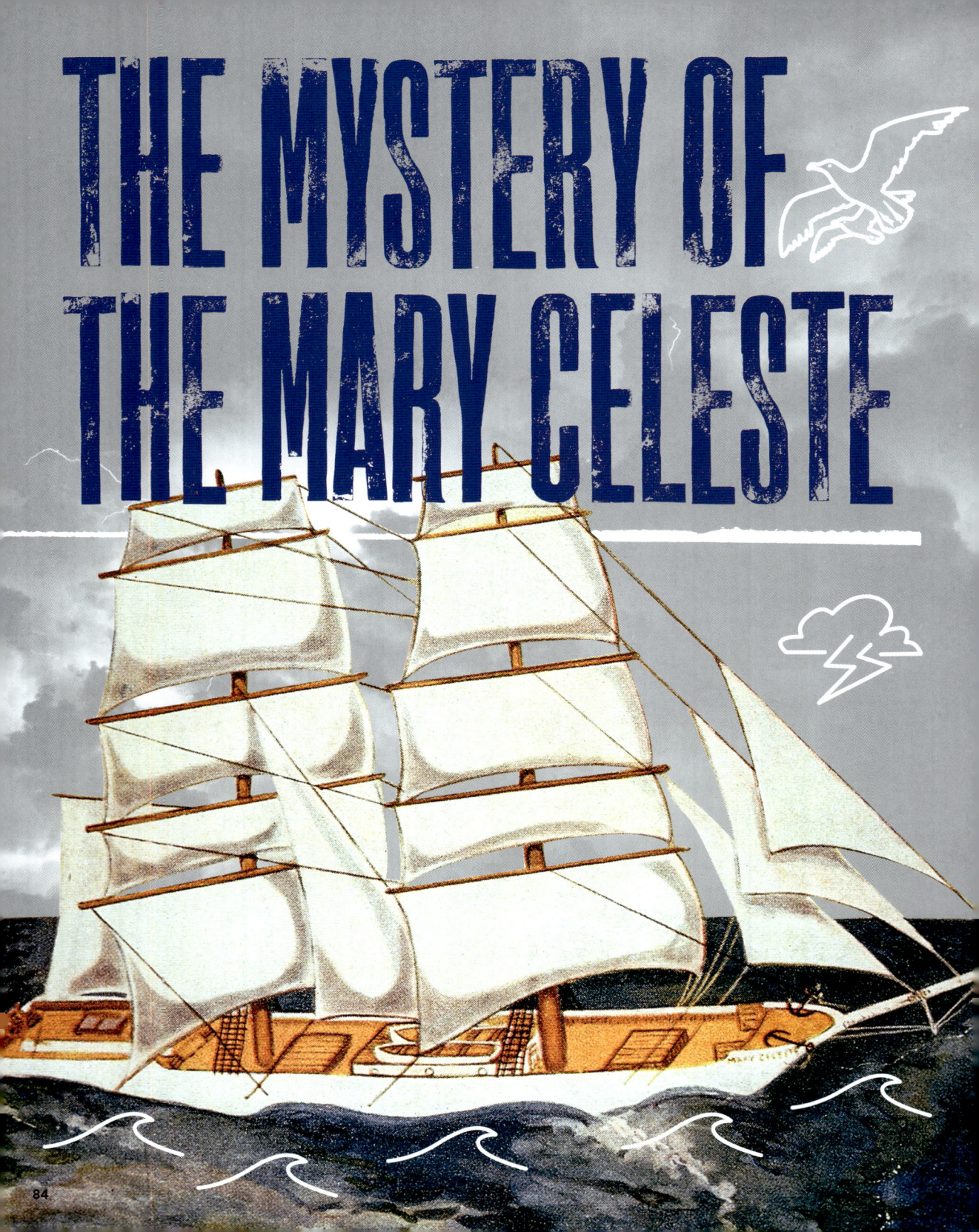

Late on December 5, 1872, a British ship called *Dei Gratia* discovered something odd. Floating off the coast of Portugal's Azores islands was a small merchant ship known as the *Mary Celeste*. This might not sound strange at first, but the crew of *Dei Gratia* knew that the *Mary Celeste* had set out from New York City eight days before them and should already have arrived at its destination. What was it doing here? Even stranger: No one was aboard.

Mary Celeste had set sail in early November to Genoa, Italy, bearing 10 people, including passengers, crew members, and an experienced captain. Captain David Morehouse of *Dei Gratia* saw no signs of struggle or distress aboard *Mary Celeste*: The passengers' belongings and equipment had been left behind, as well as all the food and water. Captain Morehouse's crew could also find no real damage that would make the passengers abandon the vessel. The *Mary Celeste* had taken on some water, but not enough to cause any danger. It seemed that the ship had been abandoned suddenly and completely. But why? To this day, the mystery of the *Mary Celeste* remains unsolved.

FUN FACT

Though the crew was missing, sailors were able to salvage the *Mary Celeste* itself. It served several more owners before it finally sank after its captain sailed it into a reef in 1885 (though no one was hurt).

Solving the Riddle

Over the years, many people have come up with theories about what caused the passengers to abandon the *Mary Celeste*. Could it have been pirates, mutiny, or murder? Perhaps a spill or explosion caused toxic chemicals to leak throughout the ship, driving people away? However, most of these theories seem improbable with no evidence of violence or severe damage. Instead, some experts think the sailors and passengers abandoned the ship because some of the ship equipment was damaged, which meant they could not tell how much water was leaking in. They may have thought they were in much more danger than they really were and chose to set out in a lifeboat. But what happened next? That remains a mystery.

LOST AT SEA

THE MISSING FLEET

By 1274, an enormous kingdom known as the Mongol Empire stretched across almost all of Asia from modern-day Ukraine through China. Its emperor, **Kublai Khan**, wanted to expand his territory even farther by conquering another land: Japan. Under Kublai Khan's orders, a fleet of nearly 1,000 ships descended on the islands of Japan. However, before the ships could attack, a powerful storm smashed through the entire fleet. Incredibly, the same thing happened in 1281, when Kublai Khan sent an even larger arsenal of more than 4,000 ships and around 140,000 men. Japan remained unconquered, and the Mongol fleet lies somewhere in the ocean's depths to this day.

THE MYSTERY OF THE WARATAH

In 1909, the **Waratah**, an Australian passenger ship, set sail from Cape Town, South Africa, on what was meant to be an unremarkable voyage back to Australia. But shortly after it departed, the *Waratah* vanished without a trace. When the ship failed to reach Australia, authorities quickly launched a rescue mission, only to find nothing. The *Waratah* and its 211 passengers had disappeared—and remain missing to this day. Some scientists have theorized that the ship could have sunk quickly due to unexpected damage, such as an explosion or a fire. Others think the ship may have encountered a rogue wave that appeared without warning. Until the ship is rediscovered, its demise will remain a mystery.

A HIDDEN HAUL

In 1594, a ship known as **Las Cinco Chagas**, which likely looked similar to the image above, was traveling from India to Portugal when it was attacked by British privateers, or professional pirates contracted by the government. The privateers bombarded the ship with everything they had, attacking it for two whole days nonstop until *Las Cinco Chagas* finally succumbed, sinking beneath the waves before the privateers could steal its bounty. And this wasn't just any bounty: According to the few survivors captured by the British, *Las Cinco Chagas* had been loaded to the brim with priceless treasures like jewels and gold. To this day, the loot—reported to be worth several billion dollars in today's currency—has yet to be found.

WITHOUT A TRACE

In 1918, an American naval ship, the **USS Cyclops**, was returning from travels to Brazil. However, as the ship entered a region of the Atlantic Ocean off the coast of Puerto Rico known as the Bermuda Triangle, it vanished. Search parties found no trace of the 540-foot (165-m)-long ship or of her 309-person crew. They hadn't even sent a distress call. What could have happened? Some experts think that the ship's cargo was too heavy, causing the *USS Cyclops* to sink rapidly. Others think that perhaps it was attacked by a submarine. Whatever the reason, the ship has yet to be found.

THE SECRETS OF SHIPWRECKS

So, you want to find a shipwreck: Where do you start? People have explored about 30,000 shipwrecks, but there are certainly many wrecks left to find: After all, scientists estimate there are more than three million shipwrecks in the world! According to experts, the best place is to start on dry land—at the library or online. To find a ship, wreck hunters track hundreds of reports on what conditions were present when the ship sank. They look at ship logs, blueprints, whether the ship sent distress calls, and what the weather and winds were like at the time. This helps them narrow down an area to search.

Next, wreck hunters use a process known as "mowing the lawn." They use technology like sonar (which uses sound waves) or lidar (which uses lasers) to move back and forth, mapping the seafloor. The hunters send these sound waves or lasers down to the floor, which then bounce back, creating a 3D image of the bottom. Other modern technologies help in different ways: Magnetometers can help detect iron and other metals that might be present in shipwrecks, while artificial intelligence can help detect changes in the soil around wrecks.

Scientists use technologies like sonar or lidar to map the ocean floor.

Some wrecks can survive for many years in the deep sea—and they can be dangerous to reach.

Wrecks found in shallow water tend to be easier to reach. Scuba divers survey the wrecks, taking notes and making measurements. But shallow water also tends to be warmer, which causes wrecks—especially wooden ships—to decay more quickly. Deep waters mean colder temperatures, which slow down the decay process. However, on wrecks in deep waters, hunters must also contend with the dangers of extreme pressure.

Who Owns a Shipwreck?

When it comes to shipwrecks and the treasure found there, like these gold doubloons recovered in the Bahamas, it's not always "finders, keepers." Some governments, like the U.S. government, have passed laws that claim ownership of the wrecks found within the borders of their country's waters. Other laws claim that the wrecks of military vessels automatically belong to the country that built the vessel.

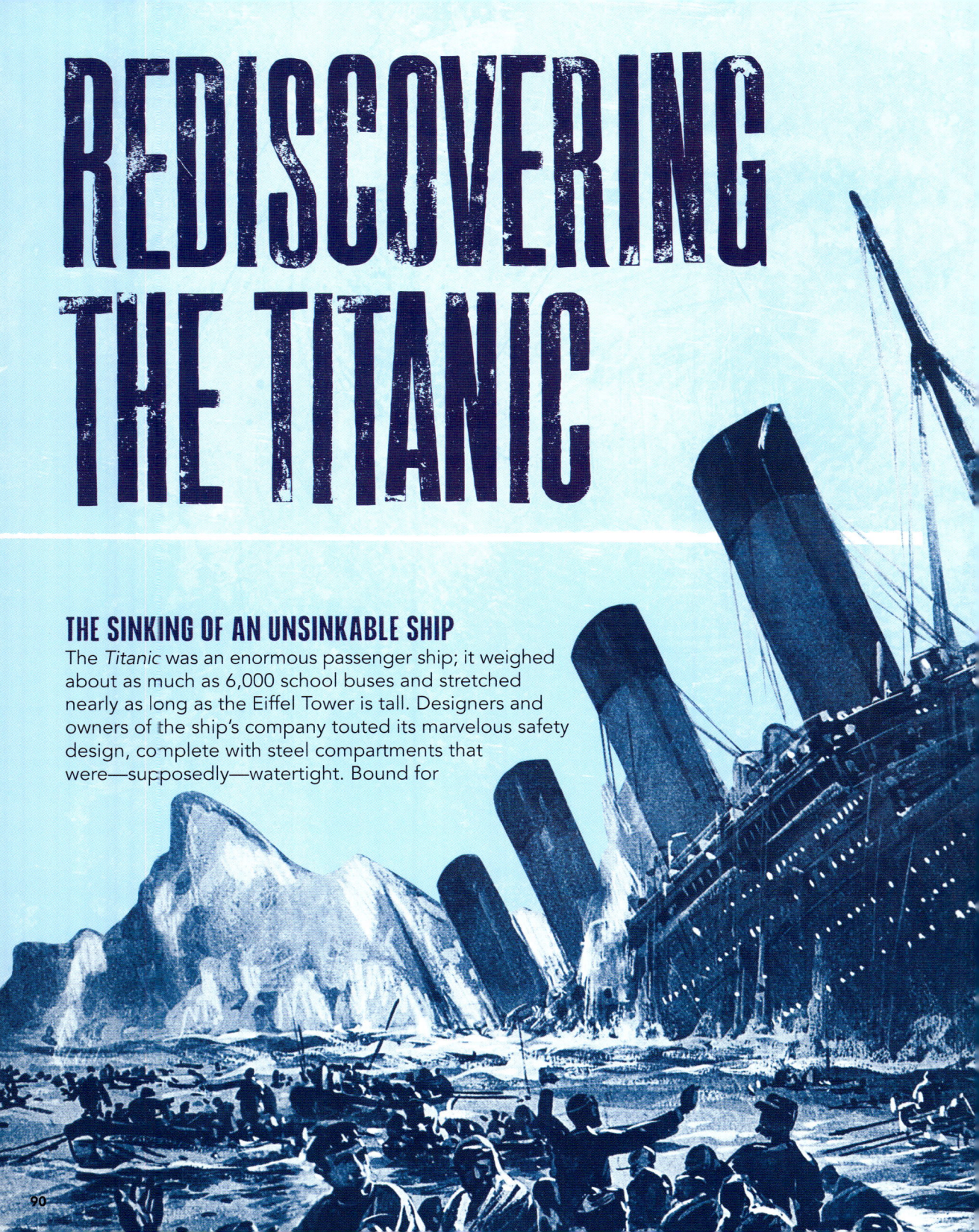

REDISCOVERING THE TITANIC

THE SINKING OF AN UNSINKABLE SHIP

The *Titanic* was an enormous passenger ship; it weighed about as much as 6,000 school buses and stretched nearly as long as the Eiffel Tower is tall. Designers and owners of the ship's company touted its marvelous safety design, complete with steel compartments that were—supposedly—watertight. Bound for

New York on its maiden voyage, the *Titanic* departed from Southampton, England, on April 10, 1912, with 2,200 people aboard. But on the night of April 14, a tragedy of errors took place.

The ship was headed straight toward an ice field, and although another ship warned the *Titanic*'s radio operators of the danger, they failed to pass the message on to the control deck. Lookouts aboard the *Titanic* also missed sight of the enormous icebergs thanks to an unusually calm and flat sea with little moonlight to see by. Normally, lookouts would search for the swells of waves against icebergs—but in this weather, the water was calm. On top of that, the ship was chugging along at 22 knots, or 25 miles an hour (40 km/h) to make good travel time. Experts considered this speed much too fast for navigating a region known for its dangerous waters. Shortly before midnight, lookouts finally spotted the deadly icebergs.

The chief officer attempted to turn the ship, but it was too late: The *Titanic* collided with an iceberg, scraping its side along the ice and tearing open the ship's thick metal walls. Icy water rushed in. Passengers rushed for lifeboats, but tragically, there were too few boats on board. In the chaos and confusion, many lifeboats were deployed less than half full. In less than three hours, the ship had vanished beneath the waters. Around 1,500 people died in the sinking of the "unsinkable ship," shocking the world.

FINDING THE WRECK

When the *Titanic* sank to its watery resting place in the Atlantic Ocean, it plunged down some 12,500 feet (3,810 m), or 2.4 miles (3.9 km)—about the equivalent of 4.5 of the world's tallest buildings lined up tip to tip. There it stayed for the next seven decades. Due to the extreme pressure and frigid temperatures of the ocean's depths, it was nearly impossible for divers to safely reach the wreck. Plus, no one was even sure exactly where it was resting on the ocean floor.

Then, in 1985, American explorer Robert Ballard led an expedition to test out a new underwater submersible machine, the Argo. This amazing vehicle was able to withstand great pressure as it dove 13,000 feet (3,962 m) under the waves—and it could even transmit images. It did not contain a crew, making it a safe method of underwater exploration.

On September 1, 1985, Argo transmitted something incredible—the first ever images of the wreck of the *Titanic*. The great ship had finally been found. Scientists sent more submersibles—including one containing human navigators in 1987—to study the formerly lost wreck. They collected small artifacts, took scans, and, eventually, even raised a piece of the *Titanic* from the depths.

An image of the *Titanic*'s front deck taken when the ship was rediscovered in 1985 (above); A small submersible explores the wreck in 2003 (top right).

TAKE IT FURTHER

What do you think exploring the deepest parts of the ocean is like? What would you see and hear? What shipwreck would you most like to explore?

An illustration showing survivors escaping in lifeboats as the *Titanic* sinks.

Mystery Solved! The *Titanic*'s Sinking

Today, scientists think they know exactly how the *Titanic* broke apart and sank over its final doomed hours. After striking the iceberg, the ship immediately began taking on icy cold water. Within three hours, the front of the boat, or the bow, was underwater. As the back of the boat raised up and into the air, it became too heavy, and the ship snapped in two. Both pieces plummeted to the ocean floor, with the bow hitting first.

But the ship went down more than 100 years ago—how could anyone today possibly know these things? On top of eyewitness accounts from survivors, scientists have also used special methods to re-create the sinking of the *Titanic*. First, experts analyzed the position of the wreck on the ocean floor, as well as tracks and marks the ship left as it slammed into the seabed. Then, they used this information to create computer-generated images of the wreck to see how the ship might have gone down in the exact conditions it faced.

A TITANIC LEGACY

Though the mighty ship sank well over a century ago, the *Titanic* tragedy still captivates the hearts and minds of many. While we will never know the full story of that fateful night, what remains on the ocean floor offers us clues.

The *Titanic*'s **foremast** collapsed as the ship sank, perhaps due to the force of the water as the ship plunged downward. While the ship sailed, the foremast would have been used to hoist flags for communication and to house the antenna wire of the ship's telegram system. Lookouts also used the foremast to access the Crow's Nest, where they could keep watch.

The *Titanic* had four **smokestacks**, all of which were destroyed during the ship's sinking. Debris from the smokestacks remains scattered around the wreckage site. Three of these smokestacks emitted smoke from the ship's engines. The fourth, however, was just a dummy added to even the ship's appearance!

At the very front of the ship was the **Forecastle Deck**. The central anchor and its chains were located here, as well as the anchor crane responsible for raising and lowering the anchor. The crew's quarters were located below. Today, it is one of the most photographed parts of the wreck.

At 883 feet (269.1 m) long and 92 feet (28 m) wide, the *Titanic* weighed approximately 52,310 tons (47,454.8 metric tons).

IRON UNDERWATER

The *Titanic*'s body, or hull, was built from iron. Today, that iron is quickly rusting underwater. Much of the ship is covered by long, icicle-like rust formations known as rusticles. Some experts think it might collapse completely within 50 years, and are searching for ways to preserve the site.

AMAZING ARTIFACTS

On various expeditions to the *Titanic*'s wreck, scientists recovered a number of artifacts like the ones shown here.

Binoculars

A pocket watch, a popular accessory of the time

A first-class teacup

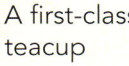

A diamond and saphire ring

A china serving plate from the ship

A black silk top hat

After the *Titanic* made impact, as water flooded the front of the ship, the rear half, or stern, lifted out of the water (as illustrated at right). The weight of the **stern** then caused the ship to snap in half. On the ocean floor, the ship's bow is about one-third of a mile (.5 km) away from its stern.

SEEKING THE COLOSSAL SQUID

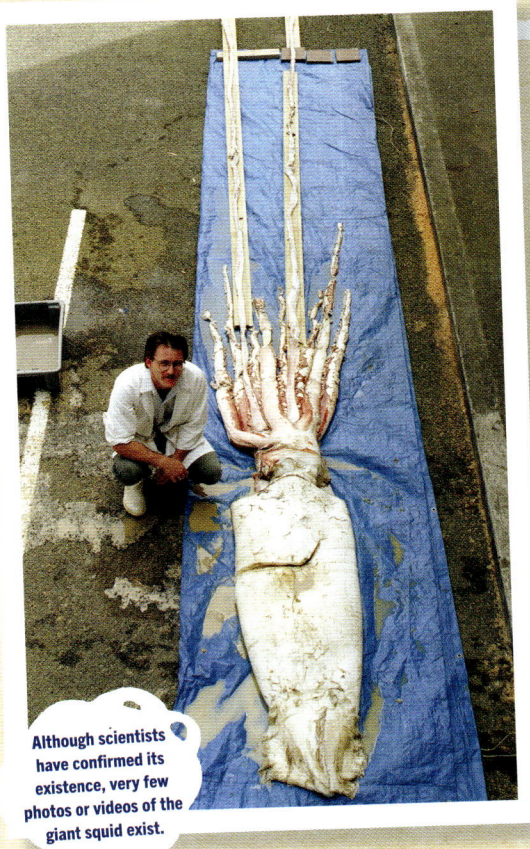

Deep in the ocean there lurks an enormous, mysterious creature: a squid so large it can battle with a giant sperm whale—one of the largest animals in the world! But until recently, scientists weren't positive that this squid, appropriately known as the giant squid, even existed.

For at least 2,000 years, sailors and fishers have told stories of an enormous, squid-like sea creature that stretched as long as 30 feet (9 m)—about the height of a three-story building. Over the centuries, people dismissed these tales as folk stories. But in the 19th century, scientists began to collect and study accounts of this "monster." They realized that it might be a real animal: an enormous squid.

Finding this elusive animal was incredibly difficult because the giant squid lives at the deep, dark depths of 1,000 to 2,000 feet (305 to 610 m). Yet there were other ways

Although scientists have confirmed its existence, very few photos or videos of the giant squid exist.

TAKE IT FURTHER

Monster Mash-Up
Experts think that giant squid may have inspired some mythological monsters. Imagine your own, entirely new made-up monster based on a real-life animal. What would the new monster look like? How would it behave?

to study these mysterious creatures. For one thing, scientists noticed that many sperm whales had scars that resembled enormous sucker marks. They believed that the whales were diving to depths to feed on the enormous squid—and the sucker marks were the result of fierce battles! Over the next century, experts recorded parts of dead giant squid that washed ashore. However, it wasn't until 2004 that a team of researchers in Japan successfully captured a picture of a live giant squid. And in 2012, Japanese scientists caught one on film!

The Real Kraken

Sailors, beware: Historians think that rare sightings of giant squid over the centuries may have inspired tales of mythical sea beasts such as the kraken, a gigantic squid-like creature said to drag entire ships to the ocean floor. Others think that a giant squid's trailing tentacles may have looked like enormous sea serpents to unaware observers.

CREATURES OF THE DEEP

Other creatures lurk in the dark, cold depths of the sea.

GHOST OCTOPUS

What's that haunting the seafloor? It's not a ghost; it's an octopus! The ghost octopus lacks pigment, giving it a pale and spectral appearance. Thanks to its home in the deep, the ghost octopus also has a soft and squishy body. Scientists think that the octopus's lack of muscles help it conserve energy in a place with little available food.

BARRELEYE FISH

The barreleye fish has a completely transparent forehead, making its two large, green eyes—and its brain—visible. The barreleye lives in the depths of the Pacific Ocean, where its enormous eyes help it see in the dark waters.

VAMPIRE SQUID

Despite its eerie name, the vampire squid isn't actually a vampire … or a squid! The vampire squid is a type of cephalopod, or soft-bodied ocean animal, that lives in deep, dark waters around the globe. There, it dines on marine snow: small bits of matter made up of dead plants and animals that sink to the ocean floor.

ANGLERFISH

This fish lives nearly a mile (1.6 km) below the ocean's surface. Though the anglerfish is relatively small (growing between about one and three feet long/0.3 and 0.9 m), it is eerie in other ways. It uses its glowing appendage to lure prey in the dark waters. Thanks to its gaping jaws, it can eat animals up to twice its own size. Don't go toward the light!

LOST

& FOUND

Enter the mysterious world of hidden objects, places, and people lost to time—and even some that have been found again!

ANCIENT LANGUAGES

LOST!

Over the centuries, archaeologists have found—and translated—hundreds of ancient languages and writing systems. But some remain a complete mystery.

PREHISTORIC CAVE SYMBOLS

At least 45,000 years ago, humans began making cave paintings that depict animals, people, and nature. Some of these paintings also include geometric symbols like circles, spirals, zigzags, and more. Recently, scientists have begun to think that these symbols may have served as a form of communication—or even as a very early form of "writing." However, it's unclear to us today what the symbols were trying to say.

LINEAR A

To many, this form of writing might look like a series of lines and scratches. But Linear A is actually a writing system used more than 3,000 years ago by the Minoans, who lived in what's now Crete, Greece. Recently, though, experts have been using computers to compare Linear A to a Mycenaean language that came later, known as Linear B. They hope that this technology might help crack the code and decipher the text.

VOYNICH MANUSCRIPT

In 1912, a historian traveling in Rome discovered a centuries-old book filled with drawings—and a strange form of writing. Known as the Voynich Manuscript, this book was likely written in the 1400s. Centuries later, no one can read it! Many scholars think the manuscript is written in some form of code. Who came up with the code and what it says remain mysteries.

MEROITIC SCRIPT

Meroitic script was a version of ancient Egyptian writing used in the Kingdom of Kush some 2,300 years ago. Using ancient Egyptian hieroglyphics, scholars in 1909 were able to decipher the writing system—that is, they figured out which symbols stood for which sounds. The only challenge? Even though they can decipher sounds, no one understands or knows the language!

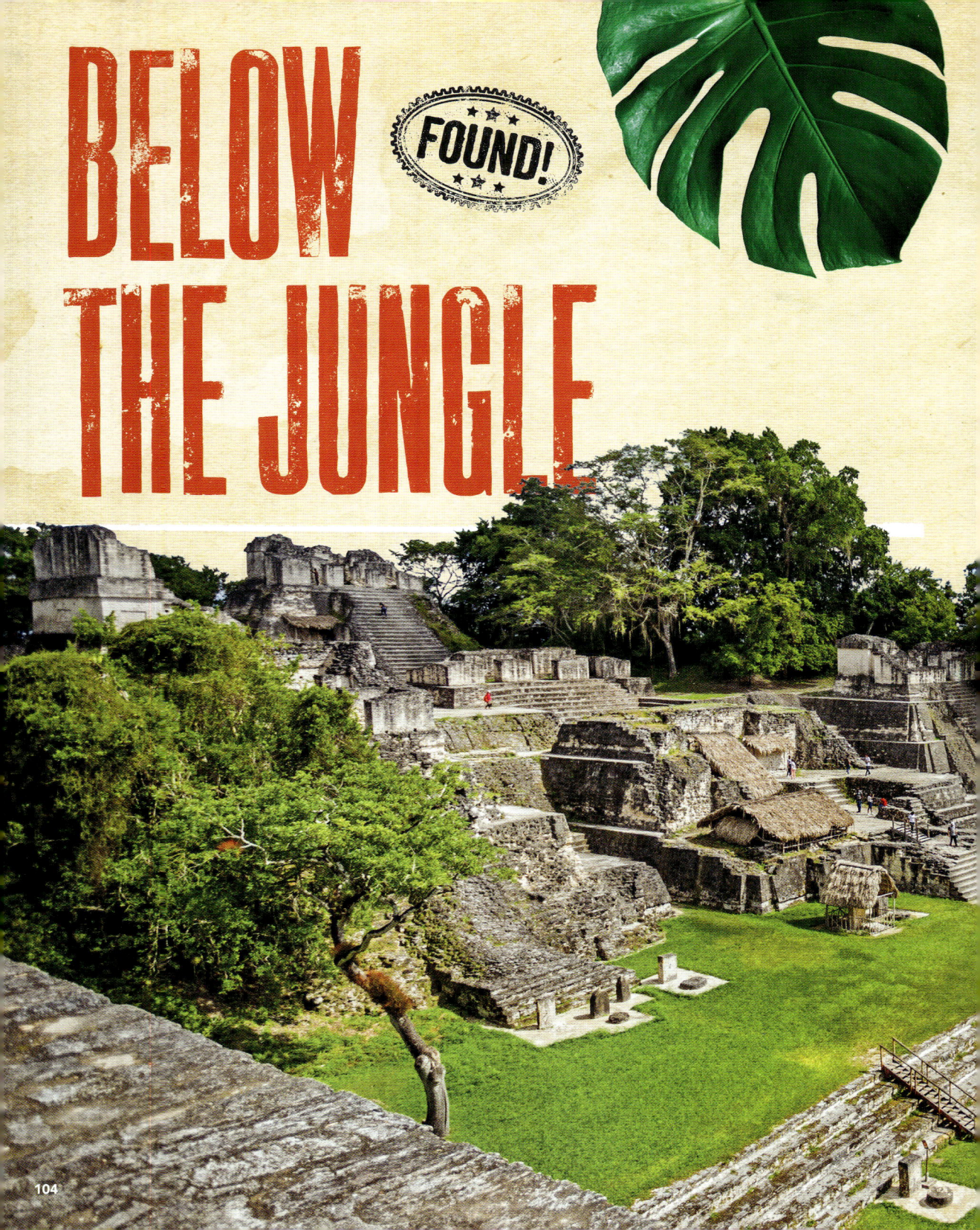

BELOW THE JUNGLE

FOUND!

A HIDDEN KINGDOM

Nearly 3,000 years ago, the ancient Maya established a city, today called Tikal in what is now Guatemala. This city in the middle of a thick, tropical jungle featured wide-open plazas, tall step pyramids decorated with elaborate carvings, and impressive stone monuments. Then around the 10th or 11th centuries, the Maya civilization collapsed for reasons that remain mysterious to us today. The Maya largely abandoned Tikal, leaving it to fall into ruin.

Over the years, the jungle reclaimed the stone city. When scientists began to study remnants of Tikal in the 19th century, almost all that remained visible were the central plaza and towering pyramids. Experts at first believed that this was the extent of Tikal. Little did they know, it was just one small part of an enormous city that lay hidden beneath the jungle floor.

This is what a finished map using a Lidar scan can look like.

Despite its location in the dense jungle, Tikal was once a major metropolis with orderly buildings (right); A large statue of a mask found at Tikal (far right).

LASERS AND THE LOST CITY

Excavating ruins in the jungle has long been difficult. The plants are thick and overgrown, making it hard to tell whether a mound might be a pile of dirt or a dirt-covered building. The jungle is also hot, humid, and home to dangerous animals, like disease-carrying mosquitoes or harmful parasites. But in the 1990s, scientists began to perfect a technology known as lidar, or "light detection and ranging." Lidar is a system that shoots out lasers at a surface, and then maps the laser beams that bounce back to form an image. These images can reveal structures hidden beneath jungle growth and layers of dirt.

Using lidar, archaeologists were able to peer beneath the dense layers of trees and plants in the jungles of Guatemala. What they found was astounding. Tikal turned out to have been not just a small complex, but a sprawling city with thousands of buildings, including houses, palaces, and even elevated walkways for moving around during rainy seasons.

What's more, Tikal wasn't the only city of its kind. All throughout Central and South America, lidar revealed that the Maya had built an enormous kingdom that was more than twice as large as that of medieval England, and more densely populated. Scientists now estimate that before its collapse, the Maya civilization contained about 10 to 15 million people. They lived in interconnected cities and used sophisticated technologies such as canals, irrigation, terracing for farming, and more.

As scientists continue to use and develop lidar, they are discovering even more cities in the jungles.

Mystery of the Maya

Around 1,000 years ago, the ancient Maya civilization experienced a sudden decline, quickly abandoning huge cities across Central America. Historians aren't sure why. Some believe this may have been due to political problems between rulers. Others think that droughts or other natural disasters may have forced people to seek safety elsewhere. And some even believe that outbreaks of tropical illnesses caused by parasites—such as one named leishmaniasis—could have pushed people from the jungles and toward the coasts.

THE KING AND THE PARKING LOT

FOUND!

Richard III of England was a man of notoriety. Born in 1452, Richard was a nobleman who loyally served his brother, King Edward IV, in court. But when the king suddenly died in 1483, Richard made huge waves. Although King Edward's son (Edward V) was the heir to the throne, Richard forcefully took the position of king from his nephew. In fact, he seized both 12-year-old Edward V and his nine-year-old brother and sent them to live in captivity at the Tower of London.

Though he was king, Richard III faced fierce opposition from his enemies at court. Rebels banded against him and killed him in battle in 1485. After that, only Richard's scandalous reputation remained—his body had disappeared. Though historians knew Richard was killed and buried, the location of his burial was lost to history.

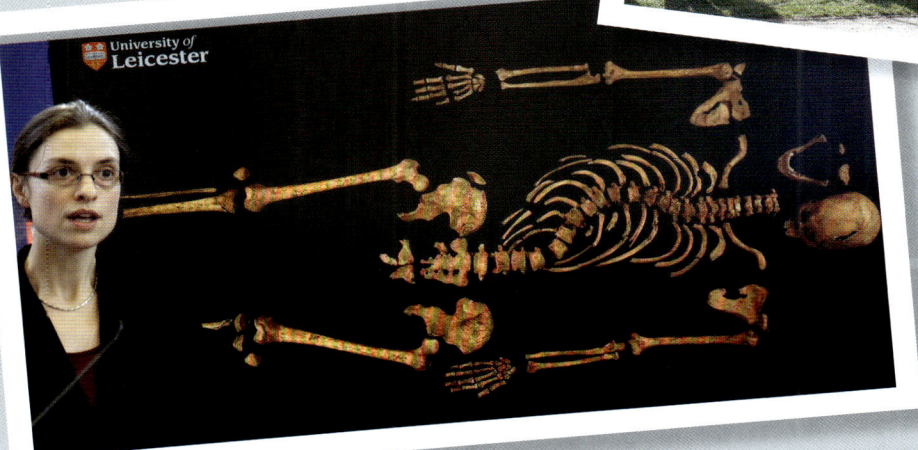

A 15th-century portrait of King Richard III (opposite); King Richard III received a royal reburial after his skeleton was discovered in 2012 (above); An archaeologist presents the discovery of King Richard III's remains (left).

Then, in the early 2000s, an amateur historian named Philippa Langley became very interested in where the remains of Richard III might be. After poring over historical documents and records, Langley became convinced that Richard III must be buried in the city of Leicester, near the castle he lived in shortly before his death. Curiously, Langley's research showed that his remains were probably underneath a city parking lot.

By 2012, Langley convinced a team of archaeologists to excavate the empty lot. To the shock of many, the archaeologists did indeed uncover a skeleton. After careful analysis, they were certain: They had found King Richard III.

TAKE IT FURTHER

What sort of research do you think is needed to uncover a lost tomb or burial spot? If you were looking for a lost crypt, what sort of information would you investigate first?

SNIFFING IT OUT

What's that smell? Who knows! Not just people, places, and things are lost—smells can become lost too.

THE WAFTS OF WAR

To bring history to life, one historian has spent time analyzing what certain historical battles might have smelled like—such as the **Battle of Waterloo in 1815**, when French Emperor Napoleon Bonaparte was defeated (at left). Smells may have included sweat, leather, wet grass, horsehair, and gunpowder.

PLANTS FROM THE PAST

Over time, different kinds of plants and flowers go extinct, meaning that no one will ever again smell their unique scents. Or will they? One company is using DNA of **extinct plants** to create new perfumes.

An illustration of the flowering plant, *Orbexilum stipulatum*.

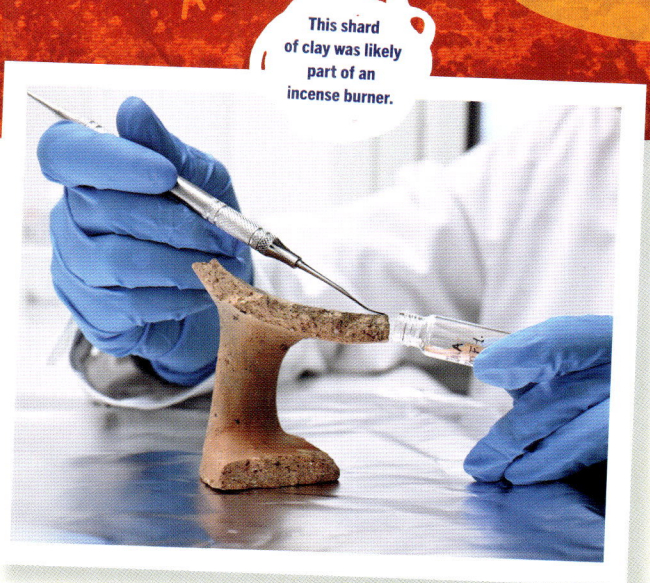

This shard of clay was likely part of an incense burner.

ORGANIZED ODORS

Founded by the European Union, a research project known as **Odeuropa** is attempting to catalog all the past scents lost to history—from the stench of a crowded London prison in 1780 to the inside of a new American car in the 1940s.

SWEET SMELLS

In Germany, one scientist is analyzing the tiny molecules left in ancient Egyptian incense holders to see if she can identify the scents. Meanwhile, in Amsterdam, historians have used historic recipes from the 16th and 17th centuries to re-create the scents in **pomanders**, which were metal charms filled with fragrance that people wore centuries ago in Europe to cover up certain stenches, such as unwashed bodies, horse manure, or rotten food left in the gutters. *Pee-yew!*

GHOST TOWNS

LOST! + FOUND!

Have you ever wanted to see a real ghost? You can—but it's not the spooky spirit of a deceased person. Ghost towns—places that were suddenly and completely abandoned, leaving only buildings and forgotten belongings—exist all over the world. Some of the most iconic ghost towns are the lost settlements of the American Wild West.

During the 19th century, miners across North America struck gold or silver in many regions (the most famous of these was likely the California gold rush of 1849). After word got out, hopeful adventurers and prospectors would rush to the locations as fast as they could. Boomtowns, communities created because of the sudden influx of workers and new jobs, sprang up. At the time, the wide-open

Colorado's St. Elmo is one of the best preserved ghost towns in the United States (above); Located in California's Mojave Desert, Calico was once a silver mining town (right).

spaces of the American West had relatively few large towns or cities. Towns tended to be far apart from one another as people often sought for—and found—precious metals in remote places.

Over the years, miners in many boomtowns, such as Bodie, California, or St. Elmo, Colorado, found that gold had started to run out. This left workers with nothing to mine—and no money to spend. And because towns were so remote, there were no other jobs to be had. People moved away to seek their fortunes elsewhere. Some gathered up their belongings, but others left them behind, choosing to abandon them rather than haul them long distances to the next location. It turned out that a boomtown could disappear almost as quickly as it had popped up.

Thanks to their far-flung locations, ghost towns often remained undisturbed. They were not in the way, so no one arrived to knock them down or build over them. Plus, many towns were in the desert, where dry air helped preserve the buildings and belongings. Today, ghost towns of the Wild West serve as eerie reminders of lost places—and as fun tourist destinations!

Ghost towns like Bodie in California, U.S.A., receive hundreds of thousands of visitors each year.

113

IS ANYONE HOME?

Abandoned places may be found all over the world—some with mysterious histories.

WITHOUT A TRACE

Sometime in the 1400s, an unknown group of people built an incredible city not far from the Indian Ocean in what is now Kenya. This city, now known as **Gedi**, is believed to have been a wealthy and advanced civilization. It contained evidence of trade with people as far away as China, as well as elaborate stone buildings and even toilets that flushed! (This was extra impressive as the modern flushing toilet wasn't invented in Europe until 1596 by John Harington). But in the 17th century, inhabitants of Gedi suddenly and mysteriously vanished. Some legends say a curse is responsible, but experts think the cause was likely drought or war.

ABANDONED AMUSEMENT PARK

The Hồ Thủy Tiên water park first opened in Huế, Vietnam, in 2004. With rides, waterslides, pools, restaurants, and more, the park was set to become a major attraction. However, costs grew and it soon ran out of money, closing its doors for good within just a few years. But the park still exists; its ruins remain, covered in vines and rust.

GHOST CITY

More than 2,000 years ago, ancient peoples in what is now Turkey created an underground city. This city was known as **Derinkuyu**, and it likely served as a place for people to retreat from attacks by neighboring enemies. At one point, the city could hold some 20,000 people. However, it was abandoned in the 1920s during a war between Turkey and Greece. Today, the city remains empty—aside from curious visitors.

FORGOTTEN FORT

Once a thriving city complex, India's **Bhangarh Fort** was established by King Madho Singh in the 17th century. The gated city contained temples, marketplaces, a palace, and more, as well as some 14,000 people. But in 1720, residents began to abandon Bhangarh, completely vacating the city by the 1780s. Why? Historians aren't certain!

FABERGÉ EGGS

LOST! + FOUND!

In 1885, the emperor of Russia, Alexander III, wanted a special gift for his wife, Maria Fyodorovna, to celebrate their 20th anniversary. The emperor contacted a Russian jewelry company called the House of Fabergé. Easter was around the corner and the jewelers concocted something unique: an extravagant white enamel easter egg that opened. Inside the egg was a yolk made of yellow gold—and inside that, a delicately carved golden hen. The hen itself opened to reveal a miniature replica of the royal crown and a ruby pendant.

Three Fabergé eggs photographed around the world: from a museum in Moscow, Russia (near right), a jewelry fair in Geneva, Switzerland (far right, top), and the Gorbachev Peace Egg in Schwabach, Germany (far right, bottom).

From then on, it became a tradition for the House of Fabergé to create exquisite, lavish Easter eggs—known as Fabergé eggs—for the Russian royal family as well as a select few other clients. The incredible creations included a pink enamel egg covered in pearl-and-diamond lilies that revealed hidden photographs when twisted; a green, leaf-covered egg that hid a mechanical bird that would flap its wings and sing; and even an egg covered in gold and diamonds that revealed a miniature gold replica of the royal carriage (at left).

By 1917, Russia was experiencing a period of extreme unrest. That year, rebels overthrew the monarchy, capturing or executing much of the royal family. In the chaos, many of the Fabergé eggs disappeared. Over the decades, some have reappeared in private collections, at museums, or even at flea markets! But several are still missing: Historians estimated that as many as 69 eggs were made, but only 57 or so have been found. That's a lot of missing bling!

TAKE IT FURTHER

If you could design a Fabergé egg with the most luxurious, extravagant material, what would yours look like? What would your egg be made of? What would you hide inside?

THE MONA LISA FOUND!

In the early 16th century, famed Italian artist and inventor Leonardo da Vinci painted a portrait of a young woman with a mysterious smile and an almost hypnotic gaze that seems to follow viewers. Today, the painting, known as the *Mona Lisa*, is one of the most famous in the entire world. But the *Mona Lisa* is not da Vinci's only painting: Altogether, the artist created many works—though today, historians have only officially found some 20 surviving pieces. Compared to da Vinci's works and other masterpieces of the time, the *Mona Lisa* is fairly small and unimposing—it is only about three times larger than a standard piece of paper, while many famous works of art cover entire walls or ceilings. So, why did this particular painting become one of the world's best known masterpieces?

A portrait of artist Leonardo da Vinci (top); The central figure of da Vinci's *Mona Lisa* (right).

For a while, it wasn't! The *Mona Lisa* was just one of many incredible works housed in France's Louvre Museum. But in 1911, a series of wild events catapulted the painting into the international spotlight. That year, three art burglars disguised themselves as museum workers and hid away in a museum supply closet overnight. The next morning, the men—including one who really did work at the Louvre—snatched the *Mona Lisa* and simply walked right out with it.

The painting remained missing for almost two years, creating an enormous stir and news headlines across the world. But one of the burglars made a fatal mistake: He had traveled to Italy, hiding the painting in a secret compartment in a trunk. When he attempted to sell the painting as a copy, the buyer became suspicious and notified authorities. Officials safely returned the *Mona Lisa* to the Louvre, where it still hangs as a star attraction and is viewed by some 7.5 million visitors a year. Of course, security is much stricter today, and involves cameras, multiple guards on duty, and even bulletproof glass.

Mug shot of Vincenzo Peruggia, the man who stole the *Mona Lisa*.

Stop, Thief!

In 1991, thieves in the Netherlands successfully managed to snag 20 paintings by Vincent van Gogh (seen at right in a self-portrait). At least, that is, until their getaway car got a flat tire, forcing the robbers to run and leave their ill-gotten goods behind. Authorities recovered the art, and soon after, arrested the thieves.

HISTORIC HEISTS

Not all of history's stolen valuables have been recovered—many remain missing to this day.

VANISHED JEWELS

In 1907 at Dublin Castle, custodians of the Irish crown jewels, a collection of priceless jewelry and medals, went to open the safe to prepare the gems for a royal visit. However, they were shocked to find the safe empty. To this day, no one knows who took the jewels or where they might be. It's a mystery of royal proportions!

MISSING FROM THE MUSEUM

Thieves disguised as police officers stole 13 invaluable works of art from Boston's Isabella Stewart Gardner Museum in 1990. The museum left blank spaces on the museum's walls where the stolen paintings used to hang (like this one beneath Edouard Manet's painting *Chez Tortoni*) and continues to offer a $10 million reward for their return.

COLD CASH

In the 1930s, American gangster John Dillinger stole some $300,000 from banks across the Midwest. Though Dillinger faced an untimely end, legend has it that $200,000 in cash (equivalent to more than $4 million today) is still missing.

BLUE DIAMOND AFFAIR

In 1989, a Thai employee working for a prince in Saudi Arabia made off with a hoard of jewels worth some $20 million—including a 50-carat blue diamond the size of a chicken egg. The blue diamond still remains lost.

MACHU PICCHU

FOUND!

During the 1500s, Spanish colonizers invaded much of Central and South America. At the time, the Inca civilization had established an empire along much of the Pacific coast in South America. Over the next several decades, the Spanish brutally captured and conquered most of the Inca leaders and population. However, survivors retreated to remote, hidden cities in the mountains, where they continued to resist the colonizers and lead rebellions for several more decades.

A tourist wanders through the stone ruins of the ancient city, Machu Picchu.

By the end of the 16th century, the Spanish had seized full control of the region, and the Inca abandoned most of their remaining strongholds and cities. Many of these cities disappeared into the encroaching jungle. In the early 1900s, American archaeologist Hiram Bingham sought to rediscover one of these lost strongholds: Vilcabamba. Bingham interviewed local residents in Peru, including Inca descendants. They told him of a tall mountaintop covered in ancient stone buildings. Could this be Vilcabamba?

Well, no. After trekking through the thick, jungled mountains, Bingham arrived at the site now known as Machu Picchu. Though it wasn't Vilcabamba, Machu Picchu was still magnificent. Set on the slopes of the Andes Mountains, Machu Picchu featured terraced farming sites, stone buildings, temples aligned to the sun's positions, and more. Though the site was not really lost—it had long been known to local Peruvians—Bingham and his team soon brought it to the attention of the world.

TAKE IT FURTHER

From the frozen Arctic to the sweltering desert, explorers search for lost ruins and scientific discoveries in the most remote places. Where would you most like to explore, and why? What type of gear would you need to explore these places?

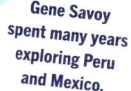

Gene Savoy spent many years exploring Peru and Mexico.

The Real Vilcabamba

Known as the last capital of the Inca, Old Vilcabamba served as a base for Incan resistance. In 1964, the American explorer Gene Savoy (at left) discovered the lost city.

AMELIA EARHART LOST!

A LEGENDARY PILOT

An early American aviator, Amelia Earhart remains famous for her incredible achievements—as well as for her unsolved disappearance. Earhart became determined to become a pilot after taking her first plane flight in 1920 at 23 years old. Just three years later, she had not only earned her pilot's license, but had also purchased her own plane.

During the 1920s, aviation was reaching new heights—literally and figuratively. Because airplanes were a relatively new invention (with the first successful flight occurring in 1903), aviators kept pushing the technology further to fly farther distances. In 1932, Earhart became the first woman to pilot a flight solo across the Atlantic Ocean. She also set seven women's speed and distance flying records, founded an organization for female aviators, became the first woman to fly solo across the Atlantic, and became the first woman to fly solo and back across North America.

On June 1, 1937, Earhart set out with her copilot Fred Noonan to break another record by becoming the first person to fly a plane all the way around the world. The pair continued their flight over several weeks, making more than 25 stops at designated rest points in more than 15 countries. On June 29, after traveling some 22,000 miles (35,405 km), they landed in New Guinea to refuel. On July 2, they took off once again. However, after several brief radio messages, the pair ceased to make contact with waiting operators. They were never seen or heard from again.

For their fateful flight, Earhart and Noonan flew a Lockheed Electra airplane, like the one pictured above. Amelia Earhart, photographed in the cockpit of her plane, at approximately 27 years old (below).

THE MISSING PILOT

Despite extensive rescue efforts—including the deployment of 66 American aircraft and nine ships—search parties found no signs of Earhart, Noonan, or their plane. Over the years, scientists, historians, and amateur sleuths have put forward many theories. Many experts believe the pair likely crash-landed in the ocean after running out of fuel, flying off course, or experiencing bad weather. Others think they may have crash-landed on one of the many small islands or reefs in the Pacific, where they likely perished. Despite the theories, no one has found the missing aviators—or have they?

In 1940, investigators found skeletal remains on Nikumaroro Island in Kiribati, a country made up of more than 33 islands deep in the middle of the Pacific Ocean. At the time, they believed the remains belonged to a male and dismissed the idea that they might have belonged to Earhart. However, recent scientists have compared the bones' measurements through an analysis software, and concluded that they very closely match Earhart's measurements. Unfortunately, the collected bones went missing years ago, meaning no DNA testing can be carried out.

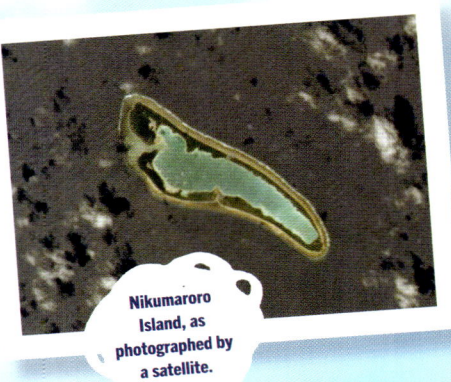

Nikumaroro Island, as photographed by a satellite.

More recently, a deep-sea exploration company scanning the seabed captured an image of what they believe might be Earhart's missing plane. Experts can't confirm or deny this until they conduct further research, but scientists think they may be one step closer to solving the mystery.

TAKE IT FURTHER

Amelia Earhart achieved many amazing "firsts" in flight. Think about which "firsts" are still left—such as being the first human to step foot on Mars or the first person to swim across the entire Pacific Ocean. Which "first" do you think would be most exciting to accomplish, and why?

North America
- Oakland 1
- Burbank
- Tucson
- New Orleans
- Miami 2
- San Juan 3

South America
- Cumaná
- Paramaribo
- Fortaleza
- Natal 4

Africa
- St. Louis 5
- Dakar
- Gao
- N'Djamena
- Khartoum
- El Fasher
- Massawa
- Assab

Europe

Pacific Ocean

Atlantic Ocean

—— Actual Route

········ Planned Route

1. **OAKLAND, CA:** Amelia Earhart and co-pilot Fred Noonan departed from Oakland, CA, in a custom-built Lockheed Model 10-E Electra on May 21, 1937.

2. **MIAMI, FL:** After landing in Miami, FL, on June 1, Earhart and Noonan publicly announced their goal of circling, or circumnavigating, the globe.

3. **SAN JUAN, PUERTO RICO:** Next, the duo headed south, stopping briefly in San Juan in Puerto Rico before heading on to Caripito, Venezuela, on June 2.

4. **NATAL, BRAZIL:** On June 6, the team arrived in Natal, Brazil, where they remained overnight to rest before a long flight across the Atlantic. They departed the next day.

5. **ST. LOUIS, SENEGAL:** The Atlantic crossing spanned approximately 1,900 miles (3,057.8 km) and took about 13.5 hours in mostly rainy conditions.

6. **KARACHI, PAKISTAN:** After zig-zagging across central Africa, Earhart and Noonan arrived in Karachi, Pakistan, on June 15. They remained there for two days to perform maintenance, leaving on June 17.

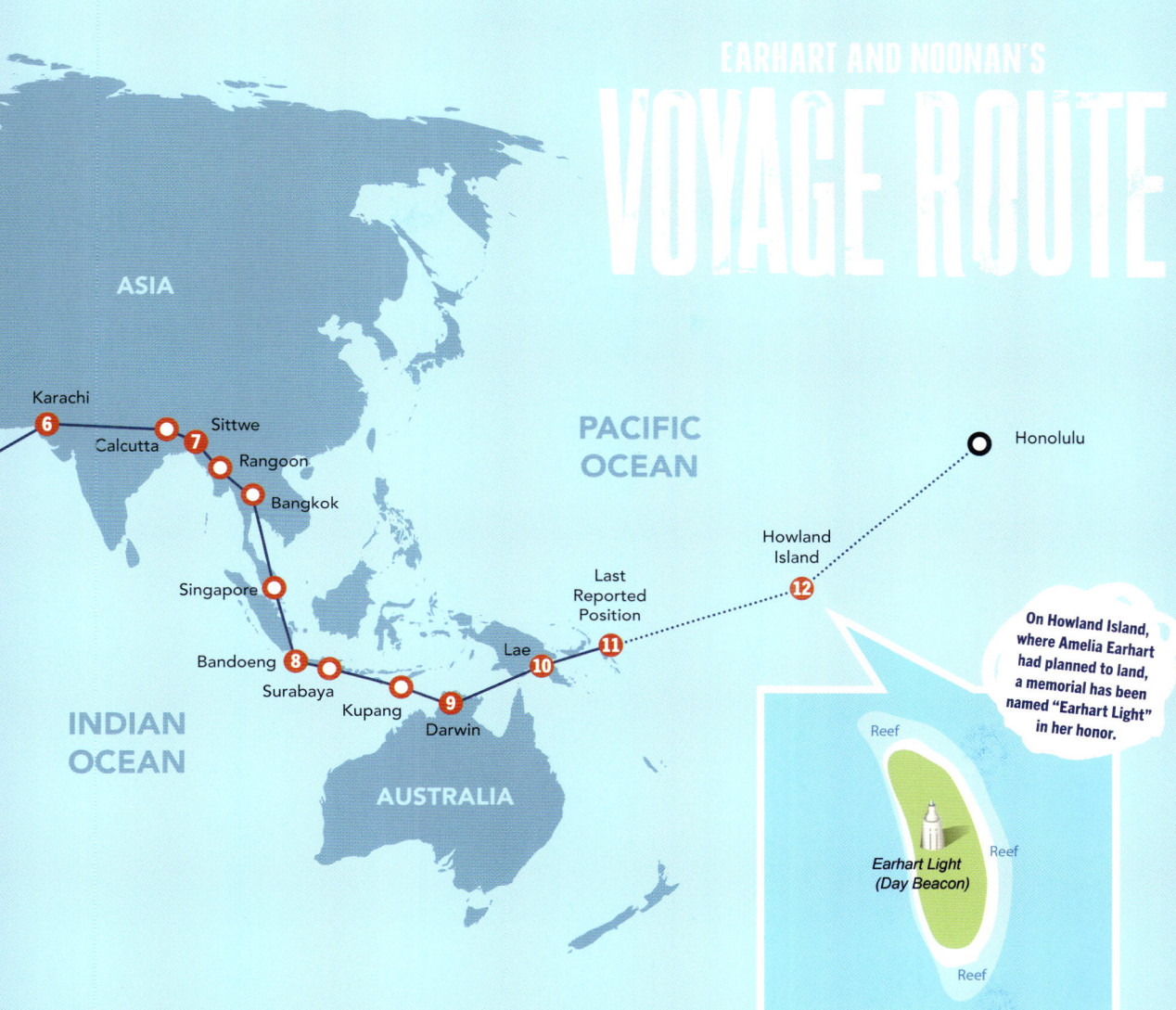

EARHART AND NOONAN'S
VOYAGE ROUTE

ASIA

PACIFIC OCEAN

Karachi
6
Calcutta
Sittwe
7
Rangoon
Bangkok
Singapore
Bandoeng **8**
Surabaya
Kupang
9
Darwin

INDIAN OCEAN

AUSTRALIA

Last Reported Position

Lae
10
11

Howland Island
12

Honolulu

On Howland Island, where Amelia Earhart had planned to land, a memorial has been named "Earhart Light" in her honor.

Reef
Reef
Earhart Light (Day Beacon)
Reef

7. **SITTWE, MYANMAR:** Upon arriving in southeastern Asia, the pilots encountered dangerous, heavy rains. They were forced to make unscheduled stops across Myanmar and Thailand.

8. **BANDOENG, INDONESIA:** Around June 21, Earhart and Noonan began to experience equipment malfunctions.

9. **DARWIN, AUSTRALIA:** After several stops across Indonesia for maintenance, the team finally landed in Australia on June 28.

10. **LAE, PAPUA NEW GUINEA:** Earhart's last official stop was in Papua New Guinea on June 29. There, she and Noonan were delayed for two days by bad weather.

11. **LAST REPORTED POSITION:** Earhart and Noonan took off from Papua New Guinea on July 2. Their last reported position was near the Nukumanu Islands off Papua New Guinea.

12. **HOWLAND ISLAND:** Earhart and Noonan were scheduled to land on Howland Island before departing for Hawaii. They never arrived.

EXTINCT NO MORE

FOUND!

Scientists have been surprised to "rediscover" some animal species once thought to be extinct.

COELACANTH

Sometimes called "living fossils," coelacanths have existed for some 360 million years. Scientists thought the fish had gone extinct along with most dinosaurs—until a scientist caught one in 1938. Forget the catch of the day—that's the catch of the century!

LA PALMA GIANT LIZARD

In 2007, the La Palma giant lizard on Spain's Canary Islands was a shocking sight to researchers—not just for its bright blue markings, but because it had been considered extinct for around 500 years.

LAOTIAN ROCK RAT

In 2005, the Laotian rock rat first caught the attention of scientists for its unusual features, including a bushy tail and a duck-like waddle. Soon, they realized it was even stranger: It belonged to a species thought to have gone extinct more than 11 million years ago! Rock on, rock rat.

BERMUDA PETREL

Also known as cahows, these birds seemingly went extinct in the 17th century. Then, in 1951, ornithologists discovered not one but 18 nesting pairs!

CHACOAN PECCARY

The Chacoan peccary, or tagua, is a bristly, piglike creature that is, in fact, not a pig. By the 1930s, only descriptions of tagua fossils existed. People thought they were extinct until a researcher spotted one in South America in 1972. Today, there are some 3,000 across parts of central South America.

THE AMBER ROOM

A reconstruction of the Amber Room is located in St. Petersburg, Russia.

In the early 1700s, Frederick I, the king of Prussia (a region in what is now Germany), desired a space the likes of which had never been seen before. Immediately, the country's top designers and architects got to work. They covered the four walls, floor, and even parts of the ceiling of the new room in amber, a beautiful type of fossilized tree sap known for its almost glowing, golden coloring. In fact, the chamber soon held enough amber to equal the weight of a large African elephant!

As if that weren't enough, the architects added other touches as well, such as gleaming, semiprecious jewels and thin layers of gold. Altogether, this personal haven—now known as the Amber Room—was worth some $142 million in today's money.

People traveled from all around to get a glimpse of the marvel. When Peter the Great, emperor of Russia visited, he was so taken with the gorgeous design that he sang its praises to Frederick I. The king remembered this, and in 1716 decided to give the entire room to Peter as a symbol of friendship. But how could one room be given as a gift? Workers carefully dismantled the decorations and structure, then shipped the pieces to Russia, where they reinstalled

the room in one of the emperor's palaces. The room, now known as the "eighth wonder of the world," remained there for more than two centuries.

In 1941, Germany invaded what is now Russia during World War II. After Nazi soldiers descended on the palace, they fell upon the Amber Room. Soldiers dismantled the gold, jewels, and glowing amber until nothing remained. They stored it in crates, perhaps hoping to sell it for a profit, and then—it all disappeared without a trace. To this day, historians aren't sure what happened to the contents of this magnificent space. Some think it was destroyed during the bombings of WWII. Others think the Nazis spirited it away on a ship … that then sank! And some think that the room's contents were sold off in small pieces. But where are those pieces? No one can say.

An Amber Room re-creation of the coat of arms of Prussian royalty (left); An artist carefully reconstructing parts of the Amber Room (top right); The Monuments Men were responsible for saving stolen art during WWII (bottom right).

Almost Lost

During World War II, invading German soldiers seized much more than just the Amber Room. All over Europe, they stole historical artifacts, precious works of art, and other cultural treasures. A group of men and women who worked as historians, curators, professors, and architects made it their mission to save as much of these works from the Nazis as they could. Known as the Monuments Men, they rescued tens of thousands of objects—such as *The Adoration of the Mystic Lamb* by 15th-century Flemish painter Jan van Eyck and Leonardo da Vinci's *Lady with an Ermine*—that might have otherwise been lost forever. These heroes worked to find the places where the Nazis had stashed the stolen objects and then returned the artifacts to their rightful countries.

MUSEUM MYSTERIES

You may have visited many different museums, but did you know that most of them have more than meets the eye? Imagine strolling through an unmarked side door and coming face-to-face with countless oddities and curiosities. You've discovered the museum's extra storage! Here, mysterious and sometimes even forgotten artifacts have been hidden for years.

A LOST MASTERPIECE

In 1924, London's National Gallery of Art acquired a **portrait of an Italian man** who had lived in the 16th century. No one thought much of the painting for nearly a century, until a reexamination revealed that the work had been made by none other than Titian, a 16th-century Italian master.

DINOSAUR SURPRISE

At the Natural History Museum in London, one **long-forgotten dinosaur skeleton** turned out to be languishing in storage. When researchers came upon the stored-away bones in 2009, they realized that it wasn't just any old skeleton; it was the fossilized remains of the oldest known relative of Tyrannosauridae, or the dinosaur group that includes *Tyrannosaurus rex*.

INSECT EXTRAVAGANZA

In the 1800s, a geologist named Charles Moore excavated hundreds of **fossilized insects**. However, in 1915, these fossils were put into storage at the Museum of Somerset, where they were promptly forgotten. Researchers in 2011 rediscovered the stash and have been hard at work studying the ancient beetles, cockroaches, and other creatures.

FORGOTTEN TREASURE

In the 2010s, a curator at London's British Museum was walking past a forgotten lump of ancient material, possibly the remains of a wooden box, when a sparkle caught their eye. Inside the lump was a **Celtic brooch** more than 1,000 years old. After cleaning up the find, the museum put it on display.

SNAILED IT!

In 1846, a **collection of snail shells** from Egypt and Greece was donated to the British Museum in London. To display them, museum employees glued the shells to cardboard. But then, four years later, a zoologist noticed something curious—one of the snails was producing mucus (something snails do to keep from drying out). The snail was still alive! When he placed the mollusk in lukewarm water, sure enough, a head emerged. The snail was given a companion and happily lived out the rest of its days.

FLIGHT 19

LOST!

On December 5, 1945, five American military planes set out from Florida. Known as Flight 19, these planes were performing a routine training exercise. For the first couple of hours, things went according to plan. But suddenly, the military base in Florida received an unusual radio message. The flight leader was worried that he and the other pilots were lost.

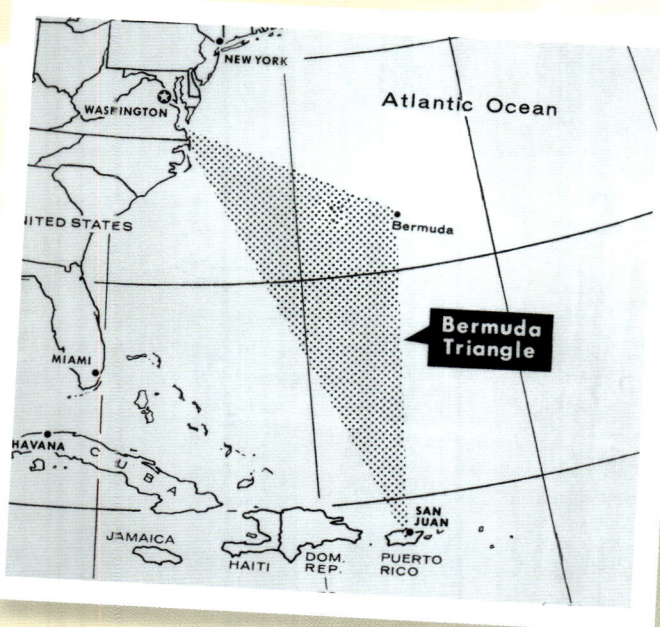

Bermuda Triangle

Atlantic Ocean

NEW YORK

WASHINGTON

UNITED STATES

Bermuda

MIAMI

HAVANA

CUBA

JAMAICA

HAITI

DOM. REP.

SAN JUAN

PUERTO RICO

Another pilot from the group sent a follow-up message. "We can't find west," he said. "Everything is wrong. We can't be sure of any direction. Everything looks strange, even the ocean." After 20 minutes, Flight 19's final message came in: "It looks like we are entering white water ... We're completely lost." The military base quickly dispatched two rescue planes to search for Flight 19. But they found nothing. Worse, only one rescue plane returned. In fact, no sign of Flight 19—or the missing rescue plane—ever appeared.

The region known as the Bermuda Triangle spans a large, triangle-shaped region of the ocean (left); Naval Air Station Fort Lauderdale, where Flight 19 departed from (above).

Over the years, wild theories have abounded. And the area over which Flight 19 disappeared—now known as the Bermuda Triangle—soon became famous for the ships and aircraft that mysteriously disappeared in its waters. Today, experts largely agree that there is nothing unnatural about the Bermuda Triangle. Even so, no one knows exactly what happened to Flight 19.

FUN FACT

According to legend, Italian navigator and colonizer Christopher Columbus reported strange sightings in the Bermuda Triangle in the late 15th century.

SOON TO BE FOUND?

Hold on to your seats: Today, archaeologists may be closer than ever to discovering some of the greatest lost mysteries in history.

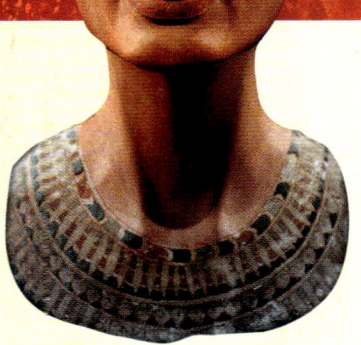

QUEEN NEFERTITI'S TOMB

Queen Nefertiti, who ruled before Tutankhamen (see p. 26), has long fascinated historians. Yet experts know very little about her—including where she may be buried. One archaeologist claims to have discovered hieroglyphics in King Tut's tomb that indicate the burial ground was originally intended for Nefertiti. Not only that; Tut's tomb may be just the outer part of a larger tomb that possibly contains the queen's burial chambers.

CLEOPATRA'S TOMB

Treasure hunters and historians alike have sought the tomb of legendary Egyptian Queen Cleopatra for centuries (see p. 40). One archaeologist thinks she may be close to finding it. Digging in the ancient, ruined city of Taposiris Magna, the team discovered a hidden, underground tunnel. They aren't sure where it goes, but they think it's a possible lead.

JOMSBORG

Icelandic folktales from the 12th and 13th centuries tell of a town settled in the 960s by famed Viking King Harald Bluetooth. Scholars have long debated whether this was a real settlement, or simply fiction. Archaeologists working on the Polish island of Wolin may have put the matter to rest: They have come upon 10th-century Viking ruins that may be Jomsborg itself.

NERO'S THEATER

Ancient Roman records indicate that Emperor Nero, who ruled in the first century, had a grand and lavish theater. It remained lost to history until 2020. Workers clearing ground for a new hotel in Rome discovered a large, ancient complex. After excavating, archaeologists have found ornate marble columns and walls covered in gold leaf, possible evidence for the long-lost theater. That deserves a round of applause!

CHAPTER 4

MYTH OR

Were these fantastic places lost to time—or did they never exist in the first place? Explore the people, places, and legends of the past, both real and mythical.

MISSING?

HANGING GARDENS OF BABYLON

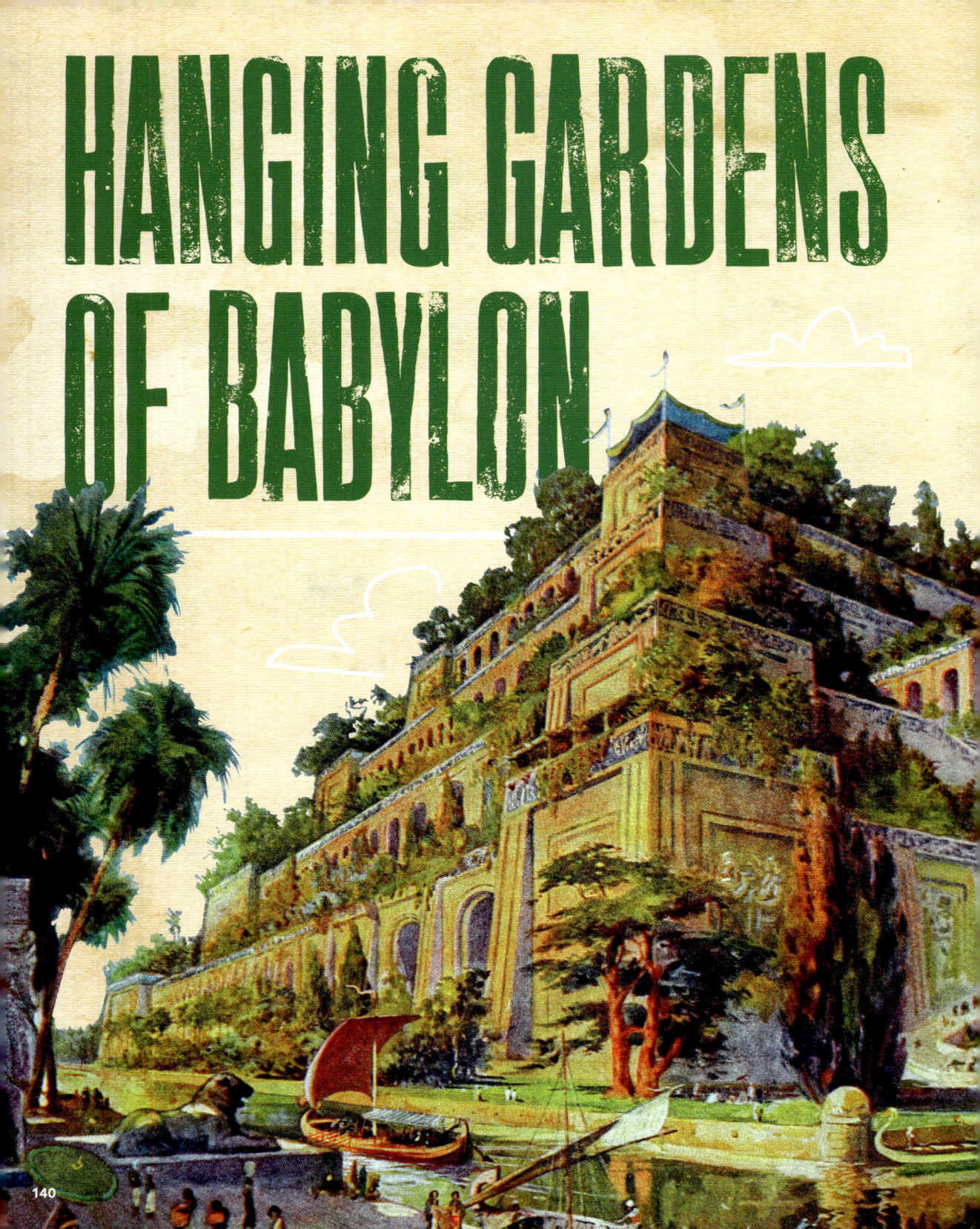

The Hanging Gardens of Babylon are famously counted among the Seven Wonders of the World (see p. 46). Tales place these gardens in the ancient city of Babylon, in what is now Iraq. According to legend, the gardens were built sometime in the sixth century BCE when the reigning king's wife, who was from a region in what is now Iran, grew homesick for the beautiful plants of her homelands. To cheer her up, Babylonian King Nebuchadnezzar ordered the construction of these gardens.

Building a magnificent garden in the middle of the desert was no easy feat, though. To water the plants, construction workers would have needed to create a huge system of irrigation in the dry desert. And since ancient records describe the gardens as a tower of plants "hanging" above its visitors, architects would have had to build marvels of engineering to carry water against the flow of gravity up the tower.

So, were the gardens real? Maybe! Historians think that the "hanging" gardens may have described a tower of terraces, all filled with plants. They think that clever engineers may well have devised ways to channel water to the tower's top. However, there is no physical evidence of any such structure existing in Babylon, and no firsthand accounts from witnesses who saw the tower. The most recent records describing the wonder appeared centuries later.

Even so, it's still possible that the gardens did exist—but in a different location! Archaeologists think the stories may have referred to gardens constructed on the orders of a different king— King Sennacherib—in the Assyrian city of Nineveh some 300 miles (483 km) away.

An early 20th-century artist's interpretation of King Nebuchadnezzar II in the Hanging Gardens.

True Babylonian Treasures

Whether or not the Hanging Gardens existed, there is no denying that the Babylonians created marvelous treasures. They produced one of the earliest forms of writing, known as cuneiform, as well as the Code of Hammurabi (part of which is shown at right), one of the oldest existing legal documents in the world.

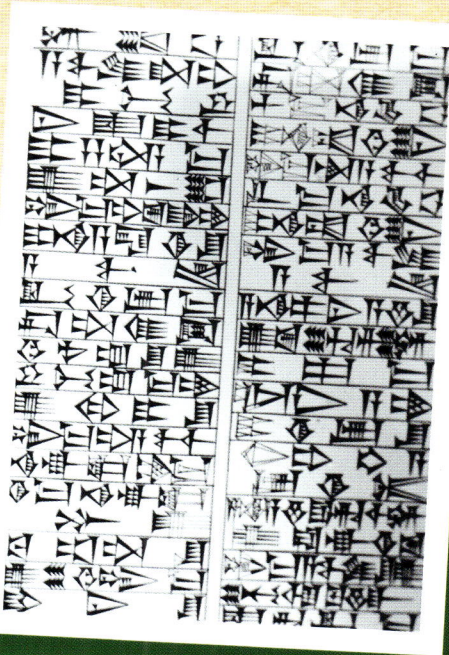

CITY BENEATH THE SEA

A map showing the supposed location of the Lost City of Atlantis.

MAKING THE MYTH

Around 2,400 years ago, an ancient Greek philosopher came up with an incredible story. The philosopher—named Plato—told the tale of a city called Atlantis, a near-perfect city located on an island in the sea. Its inhabitants were nearly perfect, too, as they were the descendants of the ancient Greek god Poseidon, ruler of the sea, sea storms, and earthquakes. These Atlanteans created beautiful boulevards, towers, bridges, and homes. The lands were full of incredible fruits, plants, and animals, as well as priceless metals like silver and gold. But, over time, when the Atlanteans grew too arrogant and greedy, they angered their gods.

Though many have imagined discovering Atlantis, no such place ever existed.

To punish the citizens of Atlantis, the ancient Greek gods sent down powerful torments: Enormous earthquakes shook the city and terrible tsunamis swept over the land. Eventually, Atlantis—and all of its inhabitants—sank to the bottom of the sea.

At the time, this tale was a made-up story meant to warn ancient Greek readers against becoming too vain or proud and angering their gods. But centuries later, when some people rediscovered Plato's writings, they took his tale as fact: They believed Atlantis was real. By the late 19th century, some scholars were arguing that Atlantis had referred to a very real place. Could that be true? Not exactly, no. While Plato made up Atlantis as part of a tale, that doesn't mean the story of what happened to "Atlantis" is altogether false.

THE REAL DROWNED CITIES

Though Atlantis never existed, countless ancient cities across the Mediterranean very much did meet their ends through devastating floods or tsunamis. Some of these cities still exist under the ocean surface or layers of dirt and ash: Archaeologists have discovered many preserved cities (see p. 72 / Alexandria), and think many more have yet to be discovered. Take, for example, the region that exists today as the Black Sea, an inland sea

surrounded by land. But more than 7,500 years ago, it was a freshwater lake. As the planet's Ice Age ended, temperatures increased and ice sheets melted. Eventually, around 6,500 to 7,500 years ago, rising waters flooded the area, sinking towns and ancient settlements.

Thousands of years later, another city in the Mediterranean also met a watery fate on what is now the Greek island of Santorini, then known as Thera. Around 3,600 years ago, Thera—which was actually a volcano—erupted in an enormous explosion. The eruption was so huge that it transformed the very lands, creating an underwater crater known as a caldera. It also set off raging tsunamis that devastated the region, sweeping huge waves over an ancient city known as Akrotiri. On top of that, Thera's ash and stones rained down on the city, burying it for thousands of years. However, archaeologists have unearthed Akrotiri and have begun to study parts of it.

Discovered in the ruins of Akrotiri, this wall painting shows daily life on the island more than 3,600 years ago (opposite page); Thera's eruption some 3,600 years ago formed the island today known as Santorini. This illustration shows a more recent eruption of 1866 (left).

Centuries later—in fact, just a few years before Plato penned his tale—tsunamis also ravaged an ancient Greek city called Helike, a powerful city that had existed for nearly 3,000 years. But after a devastating earthquake struck the land, the city disappeared almost overnight—submerged under raging waters. Luckily for archaeologists, the waters eventually subsided, leaving Helike buried in muddy dirt. Experts have been excavating Helike, and hope to learn as much about it as possible.

So, although Atlantis itself never existed, its tale was a true one for many places. In fact, some historians think that stories passed down over the years may even have inspired Plato to write his!

TAKE IT FURTHER

Over the centuries, some people have claimed to find Atlantis in strange and unusual places. Others have written books, novels, and movies about the fabled city. Why do you think the tale of Atlantis has remained so popular over the years?

Atlantis Found?

After European explorers first landed in the Americas, some scholars claimed that the "newly found" continents were the legendary Atlantis. Other treasure hunters have suggested equally unusual places where they think the city might be—such as below the ice of Antarctica, in the deserts of Morocco, or deep at the bottom of the Bermuda Triangle!

THE PHILOSOPHER'S STONE

Today, many scientists study the very small, basic building blocks that make up the universe—known as elements. This study is known as chemistry. Experts examine how different elements react with one another, and even how one can be changed into another. However, for many centuries, this idea was not known as chemistry: It was called alchemy, and it mixed science with magic.

Alchemy likely got its start about 2,000 years ago with the thinkers and scholars—known as philosophers—of ancient Greece, Egypt, and China. Some 1,700 years ago, one Greek scholar began to discuss an incredible artifact. He believed that this item, now known as the philosopher's stone, could change basic metals (like lead, tin, or copper) into valuable gold. Over centuries, the legend of the philosopher's stone grew. Alchemists weren't sure if the "philosopher's stone" was really a stone, or some combination of different chemicals and powders. However, they did believe that whoever found the "stone" would be very powerful: Not only did they believe the stone could change metals into gold, but they also thought it could bestow immortality.

Alchemists searched for ways to transform common substances into valuable metals.

TAKE IT FURTHER

Some of today's advanced technology seems a lot like magic. What other things once considered magic have been made real by science or technology?

Alchemists in medieval Arabia and Europe worked hard to unlock the secrets that would create a magical stone, but no one ever succeeded. Or did they? So far, no one has discovered a way to make humans immortal. But modern scientists have come up with ways to create gold and even jewels like diamonds. Today, experts in laboratories can create chemical reactions that cause tiny molecules to change into other substances—and form gold! They can even grow gems in less than six weeks, something that would normally take more than a billion years in nature. So, although experts have not found a magical stone, they did crack the code to creating gold. Abracadabra!

FUN FACT

In the 14th century, one French alchemist named Nicolas Flamel (at right) declared that he had found a way to turn other metals into gold. However, no one knows if this is true.

KING ARTHUR

You may have heard stories of King Arthur (shown below), who ruled over medieval Britain with his Knights of the Round Table. But did Arthur or his knights really exist? The answer is no—at least, not the exact King Arthur who stars in the legendary tales filled with magic, danger, and romance. But historians think that a real person living long ago in Wales may have inspired these stories.

The first mention of Arthur appears in a sixth-century Welsh poem called "Y Gododdin." Around this time period, the people of Wales, known as the Britons, had been fighting off an invading group of people from main and Europe, called the Saxons. "Y Gododdin" refers to a leader and impressive soldier who helped defend against the Saxons—a man named Arthur. This same man also appears in a later, ninth-century account of the Briton resistance against the Saxons. Over time, these tales grew into adventure and romance stories that featured Arthur, his queen Guinevere, a band of loyal knights, the castle Camelot, and the powerful wizard known as Merlin.

FUN FACT

According to legend, the Knights of the Round Table (at left) gathered around a round table because it made them all equal.

The ruins of Tintagel may once have been home to the "real" Arthur.

But what about the real man behind the made-up legends? Historians know little about him. Some think that the real Arthur may have lived at the cliffside ruins of Tintagel Castle in Cornwall, England. Archaeologists searching there have discovered a sixth-century inscription with the name "Artognou," which could be an early version of Arthur. However, for now, the "real" Arthur has been lost to history.

Knightly Treasure

One real order of knights, a group of so-called crusaders or Catholic holy warriors, was founded in the 12th century as the Knights Templar. By the 14th century, these Templars had become very rich and powerful, which threatened the authority of the king of France and the pope. They forced the Templars to disband, and they seized their wealth. Or did they? According to legend, the Templars had a vast treasure hidden away—and it is said to remain missing to this day.

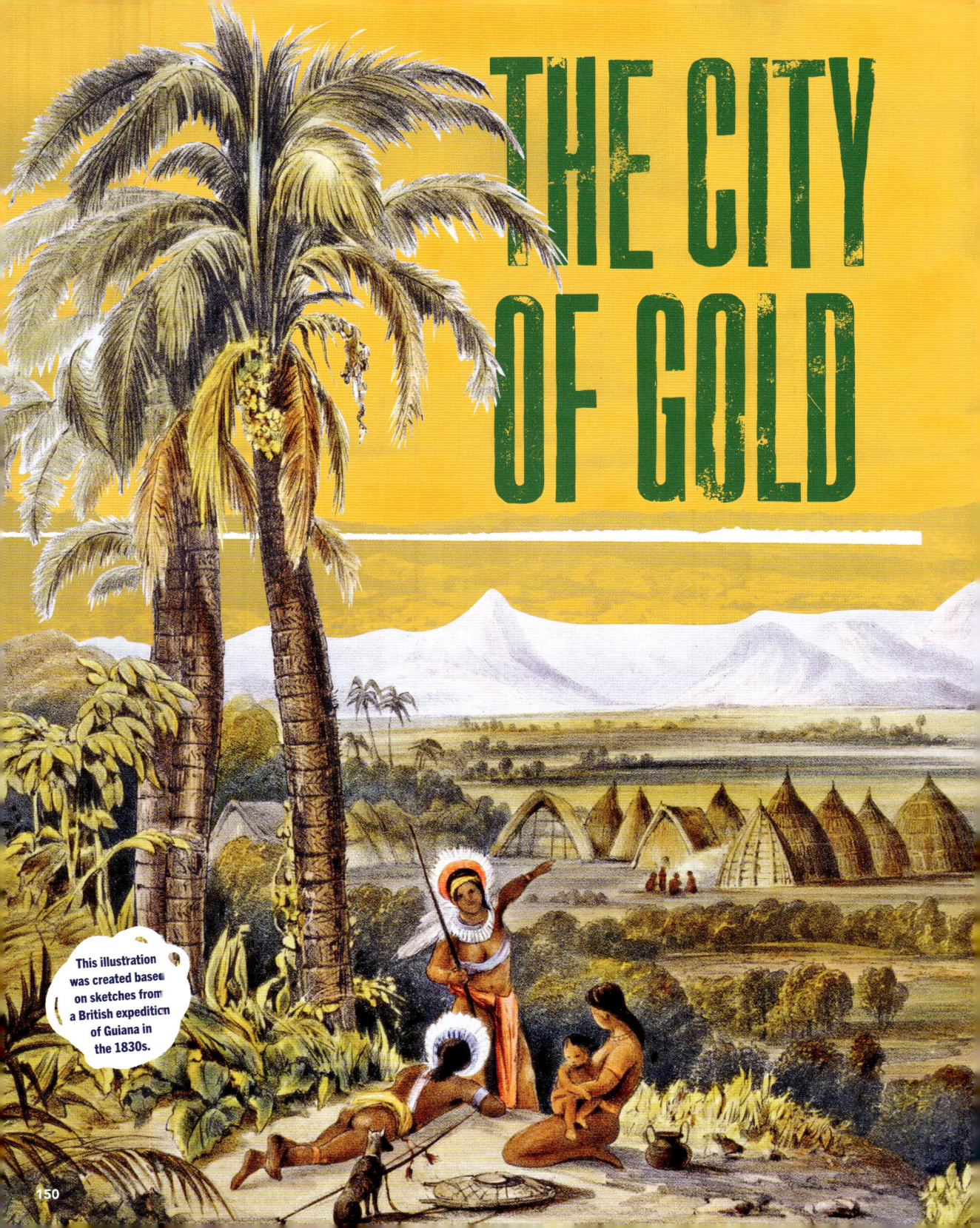

THE CITY OF GOLD

This illustration was created based on sketches from a British expedition of Guiana in the 1830s.

SEARCHING FOR EL DORADO

In the 16th century, European explorers and invaders began to share rumors of an incredible city. Hidden somewhere deep in the thick jungles of Central or South America, the city was a shining, shimmering expanse of gold. In fact, there was supposedly so much gold in this city—known as El Dorado—that even the buildings and streets were made of the precious metal. The only problem? No Europeans had ever found the city. That didn't stop them from trying.

In 1541, a Spanish invader named Gonzalo Pizarro gathered several hundred soldiers and marched through the dense rainforest of what is now Ecuador. But they found no golden city; instead, they faced only starvation, illness, and injuries. Over the next several decades, more European expeditions attempted to locate El Dorado—all with no success. Along the way, they caused untold damage and hardships for Indigenous groups across the Americas, even torturing and enslaving people.

One of the most famous searches for El Dorado occurred nearly 55 years later, in 1595. An English explorer, colonizer, and privateer named Sir Walter Raleigh assembled a crew and sailed up South America's Orinoco River in search of the fabled city, hoping to impress the queen. But he found no trace of it and returned home. In 1617, he set out again, sent by the new king who was impressed with tales of gold. This voyage ended in disaster: After Raleigh's soldiers attacked a Spanish fortress, Raleigh's son died in the battle. And upon returning home to England, Raleigh himself faced charges of treason for provoking war with Spain and was executed. El Dorado remained a legend.

A TALE OF GREED

The truth is, El Dorado, the shining city of gold, likely never existed. Instead, it was the product of greedy imaginations. Early European explorers had encountered various empires in the Americas that were highly skilled in goldwork. In fact, people living in the Americas—such as the Moche and Chavín—had been masters of metalworking for more than 2,000 years. From the Aztec to the Inca and Maya, different cultures on the American continents had produced fantastic golden art such as jewelry, masks, decorations, and more.

Raleigh and his expedition (above); Skilled craftspeople in the Americas created fantastic art from gold, wood, and other materials—such as this ceramic figure shaped like a human (below).

Golden headdresses, masks, and jewelry helped give rise to the legend of El Dorado.

When European invaders encountered this stunning goldwork, they believed that more must be hidden away. Over time, Europeans likely even heard tales of a local king who lived in a society high in the Andes Mountains at Lake Guatavita. Supposedly, this society had a special ritual: During ceremonies, the ruler would be covered in gold dust. Then, he would toss gold and jewels into Lake Guatavita as offerings for the gods. Locals called this ruler El Dorado—meaning the golden one.

Over time, eager and greedy explorers likely misunderstood this tale, turning it instead into a lost city made entirely of gold.

The Fountain of Youth

Beginning around 1100, a group of people known as the Taíno lived across many of the islands of the Caribbean, as well as in parts of Florida. One Taíno legend told of a mythical fountain that could give eternal youth to whomever bathed in its waters. In the early 1500s, Spanish explorers and colonizers brought the tale back to Europe, where it became a popular story.

THE LOST COLONY OF ROANOKE

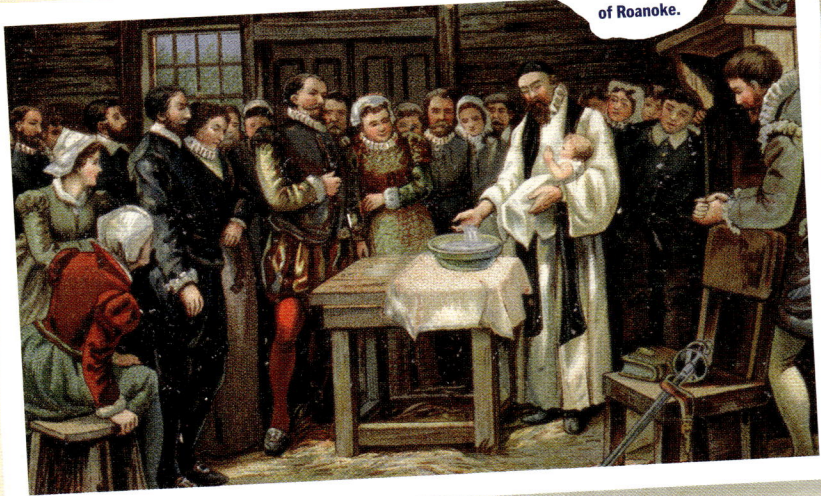

This image depicts Virginia Dare, the first child born to the colony of Roanoke.

In 1587, 115 colonizers—including men, women, and children—arrived at an island off what is now North Carolina. They had been sailing for 10 long weeks, and now, finally on solid land, they were ready to establish a new colony in honor of England's Queen Elizabeth. They called this colony Roanoke.

However, almost immediately, things got off to a bad start. The colonizers struggled to grow crops in the new climate and were often hungry. Relationships with the nearby Indigenous Algonquian nations were not good. This was in part because the colonizers invaded this "new" land, and took many resources the Algonquian people needed while also relying heavily on Algonquian help. On top of that, previous European explorers in the region had brought diseases that had left many Indigenous populations decimated, making them wary of new settlers.

Since the colony's disappearance, experts and historians have long puzzled over the only clue: the words CROATOAN and CRO written on a tree and signpost (left).

Just over a month in, Roanoke's leader, John White, sailed back to England for much-needed help and supplies. However, thanks to England's ongoing war with Spain, White was delayed in returning for three years. When White finally made it back to Roanoke in 1590, he came upon a shocking site: The entire colony was gone. Not a single person remained. All that was left were two carvings: The letters CROATOAN appeared on a signpost, and CRO was carved into a nearby tree. To this day, the lost colony of Roanoke remains a mystery.

FUN FACT

Historians aren't sure what the word "croatoan" and the letters "cro" mean. Some think they refer to the name of a nearby island. Others think it was a combination of two words in the Algonquian language meaning "council town" or "talk council."

What Happened?

Historians are stumped about the fate of the colonizers at Roanoke. But thanks to advances in technology, they have a good theory. Some scientists think that the people of Roanoke may have been killed, or else died of disease or starvation. However, experts have found no bodies at the site. Historians think it is far more likely that the colonizers split up and joined with different Algonquian tribes. Experts studying DNA of these groups' descendants hope to find proof.

This wood engraving, based on a drawing done in the late 1500s, depicts the Native American Village of Secotan in the Roanoke Island.

THE BEAST OF GÉVAUDAN

In 1764, frightening stories began to spread across France about an enormous, monstrous beast stalking the land and attacking people. In just a few years, this terrible creature had slaughtered 100 to 300 people across France's Gévaudan region. And worse—it seemed no one could stop it.

Hunters attempted to shoot the monster, and even King Louis XV got involved by setting a huge bounty on the creature's head. Luckily, by around 1767, the beast had either met its end at the hands of a hunter, or else had simply disappeared.

Today, this monster is known as the Beast of Gévaudan. But was it real? Yes! In the late 18th century, a large animal really did kill at least 100 people in France. However, historians still don't know what kind of animal it was. At the time, witnesses described the beast as "like a wolf, yet not a wolf." Witnesses claimed that the creature was larger than a wolf, and perhaps even as large as a horse. Others described it as having reddish fur, a long, tufted tail, and a fuzzy, black stripe down its back. It also had long, sharp claws.

FUN FACT

Beware of the moon: Some people of the 18th century believed the Beast of Gévaudan was a werewolf!

TAKE IT FURTHER

Some experts think the beast was a young lion—and that the descriptions of the Beast of Gévaudan came from people who had never seen one before. How do you think people might describe animals they've never seen before? How might a person who has never before met a dog describe one?

Based on these descriptions, some scholars have theorized that the beast may have been a young male lion. Juvenile male lions don't yet have manes; instead, they have a slightly reddish color with black tufts of fur on their back. Perhaps a lion brought to Europe escaped from captivity and went on to terrorize the people living in the Gévaudan region. We may never know for sure.

In this illustration, the citizens of Gévaudan fight back as "the beast" attacks.

COOL CRYPTIDS

For centuries, people across the world have claimed to spot incredible, animal-like creatures previously unknown to science. These animals are known as cryptids. Could they really exist?

YETI

Like Sasquatch, the Yeti (also sometimes called the Abominable Snowman) is an ape-person cryptid. However, the Yeti supposedly makes its home in the snowy climate of the Himalaya mountain range.

Scientists think that legends of Yeti may have been inspired by bears living in the mountains.

OLGOI-KHORKHOI

For centuries, Mongolian tales have mentioned an enormous, predatory worm that slithers under the sands of Asia's Gobi desert. Known as the Olgoi-Khorkhoi or the Mongolian death worm, it supposedly reaches lengths of up to seven feet (2.1 m),

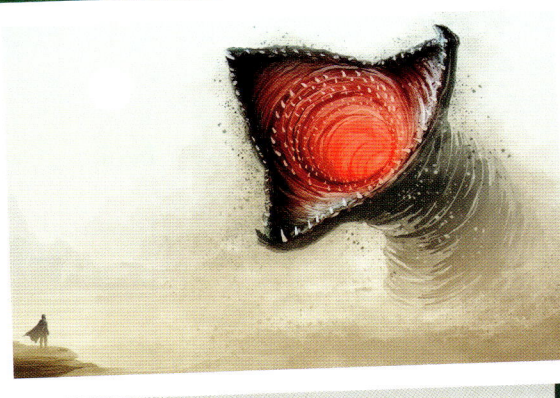

or longer than an adult is tall. Tales of the deadly worm may even have served as the inspiration for the enormous sandworms in the science fiction series *Dune*.

QALLUPILLUIT

In Inuit tales that have been told for centuries, Qallupilluit are humanlike ocean creatures feared for luring children to their deaths in icy waters. These monsters may not be based on any real animals—rather, they may serve as warnings to children to stay away from dangerous areas.

SASQUATCH

What's that lurking in the woods? One of the most popular crytpids, Sasquatch—also known as Bigfoot—is said to be a humanlike ape that roams the forests of western North America. Tales of Bigfoot have appeared in myths of various cultures for centuries, and have even cropped up in the writings of Spanish colonizers (in what is now California) in the 1600s.

CITY IN THE DESERT

Spanning much of northern Africa, the Sahara is a vast and deadly desert. It has little accessible water, and relatively few animals call the region home. But in the 19th century, rumors began to swirl across Europe: Supposedly, the Sahara was the site of a long-lost city. Once a magnificent oasis, the stone city had since been swallowed by the desert sands.

Almost nothing is known about this supposed city, Zerzura. Historians aren't even sure when the legend originated. In the 19th century, an explorer and writer who was spending time in northern Africa wrote a book of what

Zerzura supposedly existed at an oasis—a fertile spot in the desert where water can be found (left); This rock formation is from a desert in Namibia, a country in southern Africa (below); Golden sand dunes in the Sahara Desert (opposite bottom).

he claimed were tales and accounts from local people living in Egypt and Libya. According to him, these people spoke of a once shining city hidden in the sandy dunes, filled with treasure. But was this city real?

The only documentation that Zerzura existed supposedly comes from a 15th-century text known as the Kitab al Kanuz. In the text, the author describes Zerzura as a large oasis full of palm trees and natural springs. Large stone blocks made up the buildings, and a statue of a bird guarded the front gate entrance. When a person approached, the bird statue was said to drop a key into their waiting hands. However, there's a catch: No Kitab al Kanuz exists outside of that one passage. In fact, no one knows who the author even is. Based on the loose accounts and lack of any evidence, experts think the story of Zerzura is simply a tall tale told over time.

TAKE IT FURTHER

Why would an explorer make up a tale about discovering a lost city? Try coming up with your own story about a vanished kingdom.

Making a Myth

For more than a century, explorers have searched for another lost desert city: The Lost City of the Kalahari was supposedly hidden in the vast red sands of the Kalahari Desert in southern Africa. Only one person has ever claimed to have seen the city. In 1885, Canadian explorer William Leonard Hunt supposedly came upon incredible ruins of curved stone walls. However, many modern historians think Hunt probably mistook a natural rock formation for man-made ruins. And others think he just made up the whole story!

THE LOST CITY OF Z

In the early 1900s, British explorer Percy Fawcett was visiting South America when he began to hear local tales of an ancient city. Supposedly, this city—which Fawcett came to call the "Lost City of Z"—was once the home of a grand and technologically advanced society. However, it had since vanished as if the Amazon jungle had swallowed it whole. Fawcett became determined to find Z. He pored over the accounts of 18th-century European explorers, who mentioned coming upon enormous stone cities, temples, and even hieroglyphic writings in the dense jungle.

Explorer Percy Fawcett in 1925 (top); The Amazon rainforest (bottom).

Fawcett mounted six expeditions to the Amazon, but each time was forced to turn back because of terrible conditions. Finally, in 1925, Fawcett set out for a seventh—and final—expedition. Joined by his son and a fellow explorer, Fawcett disappeared into the jungle in search of Z. The three men were never seen again. To some outsiders, it seemed that Fawcett's search had been in vain, and that the Lost City of Z was nothing more than a fantasy like so many other lost legends. However, Z may have been very real—and it may no longer be missing.

Percy Fawcett ventured into the depths of the Amazonian jungle, but never returned.

The same year that Fawcett disappeared, another team of Western archaeologists "discovered" an ancient Amazonian city (though locals had long known of the ruins). Because of the dense jungle and dangerous conditions, the city hadn't been studied until recently, when scientists could take advantage of new technologies like lidar (see p. 107). Historians estimate that this city—known as Kuhikugu—likely appeared around 1,500 years ago. With its wide boulevards and sophisticated planned spaces, it very well may have been Fawcett's Lost City of Z.

What Happened to Percy Fawcett?

After Fawcett's team went missing, multiple rescue expeditions attempted to track them down. None were successful. Over the years, as many as 100 people may have died or gone missing following in Fawcett's footsteps. Though this may seem shocking, the Amazon jungle hosts any number of dangers, from wild animals to parasites, treacherous terrain to limited food and water. Fawcett's exact fate will likely remain a mystery.

THE ROSWELL INCIDENT

In 1947, a rancher in Roswell, New Mexico, U.S.A., was driving across his land when he found something strange: a pile of wreckage scattered across the ground. Even stranger, this wreckage was like nothing he had ever seen before. It seemed that a metallic-looking, flying vehicle had crash-landed on his ranch. Unsure of what to do, the rancher turned in his find to the local sheriff, who then contacted a nearby army base.

After collecting the wreckage, officers from the U.S. military announced that the wreckage was part of an alien spacecraft that had crashed into the New Mexico desert. The shocking news quickly caused an uproar. Attempting to backtrack, the military then claimed that the item had, in fact, simply been a man-made weather balloon. However, this only fueled the alien rumors, as investigators could clearly tell that the wreck was not that of a weather balloon. Soon, rumors swirled that a government cover-up was hiding alien life.

In truth, the military was attempting a cover-up—but not to hide extraterrestrial visitors. The flying disk had actually been a classified high-altitude balloon that the U.S. Army was testing. The balloon was part of a secret spying program known as Project Mogul. In their haste to cover up their classified work, U.S. officials accidentally created one of the most enduring alien myths in the country!

An Army intelligence officer sorts debris from the Roswell crash site (above).

TAKE IT FURTHER

If intelligent life does exist elsewhere in the universe, what do you think it looks like? Describe where you think it lives and how it acts.

Could Aliens Exist?

Many scientists agree that it is very likely—given the incredible size of the universe—that life exists beyond Earth. Some of this life could even be intelligent. However, these "aliens" likely wouldn't look like the aliens of science fiction. Many might even be microbes, or tiny, simple organisms.

THE HOAXES OF HISTORY

Some discoveries change the course of history. Others turn out to be hoaxes—or purposeful fakes meant to trick people into thinking they are real.

FAKE FAIRIES

In 1917, two young girls in the U.K. staged photos of themselves with "**fairies**" made from paper cutouts. These faked photos caught the eye of local believers—including Sherlock Holmes author Arthur Conan Doyle—and soon appeared in international newspapers.

LURING THE LOCH NESS MONSTER

Since the seventh century, people have been telling tales of a giant marine monster living in Scotland's **Loch Ness**. In 1933, a self-styled monster hunter arrived to catch the beast, claiming to discover enormous footprints. The next year, another person snapped a photo of what looked like an ancient plesiosaur (see p. 63) lurking in the lake. The only problem—it was all faked.

MISSING LINK

In the early 1900s, an amateur geologist in England discovered the **fossilized skull** of an ancient species of early human. This find seemed to prove a close relation between apes and early humans. However, when scientists reexamined the skull in the 1950s, they found it to be fake: Someone had purposefully merged parts of a human skull and that of an orangutan.

SEEING DOUBLE

In the 19th and early 20th centuries, some people in western Europe and the United States claimed that they were "**mediums**," or people who could communicate with spirits and ghosts. One medium said he could capture the images of ghosts on film. But don't let your eyes fool you; in reality, he was reusing film to cause faint double images to appear in one photo.

TAKE IT EVEN FURTHER

Bring history—and its lost mysteries, secrets, and legends—to life with these fun activities.

PRESERVE YOUR MEMORIES

Throughout millennia, humans have been creating lavish tombs or using natural preservation methods—like marshy bogs—to keep their memories alive. Create a cool time capsule of your own memories, then set a date in the future to open it!

You Will Need

☐ container
such as an empty paint can with a lid, a shoebox, or a plastic snack bin

☐ photos, letters, mementos

☐ paper   ☐ pen or pencil

☐ permanent marker

1. **Collect your mementos.** These can be anything from photographs and letters to ticket stubs, drawings, small toys, key chains, and more.

2. **Write a letter to a person in the future.** This can be any person—including yourself! What would you want people in the future to know about you? What would you want to remember about how your life is now?

3. **Place your items in the container.** Use a permanent marker to write the current date on the container.

4. **Bury your time capsule.** If your container is airtight (like a plastic snack bin), have an adult help you bury it in an allowed place outside. If not, find a cool, dry place to store it.

5. **Check in.** Set a reminder on your calendar to look through the items in your time capsule and see how you have changed!

DESIGN A PIRATE PERSONA

Take inspiration from the pirate legends of the past to design your own pirate alter ego.

You Will Need

☐ Large sheet of paper, card stock, or cardboard

☐ paints, markers, or crayons

1. **Give yourself a pirate name.** Use the instructions below, or come up with a name of your own choosing!

TAKE THE LAST DIGIT OF THE YEAR YOU WERE BORN:

0 = Swashbuckling
1 = Bloodthirsty
2 = Pistol
3 = Notorious
4 = Plank-walking
5 = Captain
6 = Barnacle
7 = Scarlet
8 = Raging
9 = Blackhearted

CHOOSE YOUR FAVORITE ANIMAL:

Wolf = Sea Wolf
Tiger = Terrible
Shark = Fierce
Panda = Cuddly
Dolphin = Swift
Horse = Wise
Pig = Clever
Cat = Mysterious
Dog = Loyal
Bird = Plunderer

_____   _____   THE   _____

[answer 1]   [your first name]   [answer 2]

2. **Craft your pirate legend.** Would you want to be feared? Respected? Mysterious? Decide what your goal as a pirate would be: Wealth? Adventure? Or something else? How would you dress, and what sort of rumors would you start to achieve your goal?

3. **Design a wanted poster for yourself!** You can't be a pirate without causing some trouble! What are you wanted for? What bounty is being offered?

CREATE A CODE

People and places aren't the only things lost to history—languages are too! Experts spend lots of time trying to decode these languages. Get in on the action by creating your own code! Write the alphabet from A to Z in a grid like the one below. Then, design a simple symbol to replace each letter. Each symbol should be different from the others. Now write a message using your code!

A	B	C	D	E	F	G	H	I
J	K	L	M	N	O	P	Q	R
S	T	U	V	W	X	Y	Z	

PLAN A SPECTACULAR CITY

Historians and scientists have discovered incredible cities and towns that have been lost to time. But there have also been tales of cities that never existed! Draw a picture or write a story about a brand-new mythical city. What is this city made of? Who lives there?

DESIGN YOUR OWN LOST DINOSAUR

When scientists first began to study dinosaurs, many paleontologists made mistakes about how these creatures might have looked or acted. Now, it's your turn to create a mixed-up dino! Try mixing and matching features from your favorite dinosaurs (check out the ones below for inspiration!). Or start with an image of parts of a dinosaur fossil and imagine how the dinosaur might have looked. Don't forget to give it a name too!

INDEX

PHOTO CREDITS

Library of Congress Cataloging-in-Publication
Data Available on request

10 9 8 7 6 5 4 3 2 1

Published by Hearst Home Kids, an imprint
of Hearst Books/Hearst Magazine Media, Inc.
300 W 57th Street
New York, NY 10019

Jacqueline Deval, VP, Publisher
Zach Matthews, Group Creative Director
Nicole Fisher Deputy Director
Maria Ramroop, Deputy Managing Editor

Produced by WonderLab Group LLC
Lisa M. Gerry, Project Manager
Paige Towler, Writer and Researcher
John Foster, Designer
Jill Foley, Photo Editor
Annika Robbins, Fact-checker
Heather McElwain, Copy Editor
Lori Merritt, Proofreader
Connie Binder, Indexer

For information about custom editions,
special sales, premium and corporate
purchases: hearst.com/magazines/hearst-books

Printed in China
978-1-958395-65-3

Explore more puzzling mysteries
and fascinating discoveries! Scan
the QR code for the latest stories
from *Popular Mechanics*.